GETTING ME CHEAP

GETTING ME CHEAP

How Low-Wage Work Traps
Women and Girls in Poverty

**Amanda Freeman
and Lisa Dodson**

THE
NEW
PRESS

NEW YORK
LONDON

Requests for permission to reproduce selections from this book should be made
through our website: https://thenewpress.com/contact.

Published in the United States by The New Press, New York, 2022
Distributed by Two Rivers Distribution

ISBN 978-1-62079-742-2 (hc)
ISBN 978-1-62097-771-2 (ebook)
CIP data is available

The New Press publishes books that promote and enrich public discussion and
understanding of the issues vital to our democracy and to a more equitable world.
These books are made possible by the enthusiasm of our readers; the support of a
committed group of donors, large and small; the collaboration of our many partners
in the independent media and the not-for-profit sector; booksellers, who often hand-
sell New Press books; librarians; and above all by our authors.

www.thenewpress.com

Book design and composition by Bookbright Media
This book was set in Sabon and Interval Next

Printed in the United States of America

10 9 8 7 6 5 4 3 2 1

Contents

Authors' Note

In 2019, before the pandemic, the Brookings Institution released a report describing the low-wage workforce: the roughly 53 million Americans making an average of $10.22 an hour, or essentially poverty incomes.[1] This is the part of the U.S. labor market disproportionately relegated to women, disproportionately Black, Latinx, and immigrant workers. Over the two years that followed, as the pandemic unfolded, it was clear these same women would be the workers who suffered the most. Jerome Powell, chair of the Federal Reserve, put it like this, in the spring of 2020: "The people getting hurt the worst are . . . the lowest paid people. It's women to an extraordinary extent."

At the time Powell made that statement, we had been listening to low-wage moms for years. So we were not surprised that the pandemic took the most from those who could least afford it. This is not new. Low-wage women work in food services, as grocery clerks, and in retail sales; as cleaners and childcare workers; and in the rapidly expanding market for home health–, elder-, and personal-care work. The nation's backwater jobs are largely filled by women—and disproportionately by Black and Brown women. While raising more than half of all kids in America, these women provide the services that higher-income people rely on to manage career and family demands. They work to uphold the comfort and well-being of the affluent but are left to care for their own children and families on poverty earnings.

As one woman put it to us years ago, "They get me cheap."

This book is guided by the concerns and values that low-income women emphasized and circled back to repeatedly in our conversations with them. It is not a linear story nor one molded by current partisan debates. Instead, it mirrors the lives these women described to us, multitasking and shapeshifting above all, in order to be there for their kids. We heard how they changed jobs, went back to school, joined the armed services, made residential moves, and at times sought public aid to supplement poverty pay. Across states and over the years, one thing never changed. Motherhood and kids always remained at the center of their lives.

Hearing from Working Poor Women

Over the last ten years, we have been involved in a variety of research projects that were designed and developed with the participation of low-income women.[2] All of the projects also included collaborating with a local, statewide, or national organization committed to economic equity for working poor women, their families, and communities. These organizations' networks and, above all, their trustworthiness among low-income, BIPOC, and immigrant communities were absolutely essential to our work. Importantly, our trustworthiness was requisite as well and we were vetted before being invited to reach out to or meet with low-income women in these networks. Additionally, in developing our research approach, we tried to recruit diverse research teams that included low-income women with personal experience on the issues central to the projects.

In all, we talked with 250 low-income mothers who identified as African American or Black, white, Latinx, "mixed
race," and a small number who identified as Native or Native
American. Our research took place in Massachusetts, Colorado, Delaware, Michigan, Oregon, Georgia, Pennsylvania, New York, Washington, and Connecticut. We gathered
information using two common research methods: face-to-
face interviews and focus groups, the latter of which we refer
to here as group discussions and community conversations.
The interview approach varied; in some cases we met with a
woman once and in other cases several times. We met in their
homes, playgrounds, schools, or sometimes local program
offices. We also used phone interviews, given moms' overbur-
dened schedules, and then, during the pandemic, switched
entirely to phones.

The focus groups or community conversations were held in
local settings like community centers, churches, and schools,
usually gathering to talk around a table. In most cases, moms
were meeting each other for the first time. But often they found
connections through neighborhood ties and their kids' social
networks. In contrast to individual interviews, these group
conversations were largely unstructured and led by the issues
parents raised. Like the interviews, the conversations invariably circled around children's well-being, schooling, childcare
issues, and a lot of discussion about jobs and public assistance,
as well as immediate health and family concerns. We provided childcare and a meal, as needed, when meeting in person.
When possible, we compensated participants for their time
with a store gift card or cash. Reflecting human subjects' protections, the real names and identifying details of the women

have been changed, and participants were urged to skip any question that they did not want to answer.

Where We Fit In

It was shared history that led us to work together, over fifteen years ago, in the Sociology Department at Boston College, as research professor and graduate student—both of us white women. When we met at Amanda's graduate student orientation, Lisa was struck by the fact that Amanda introduced herself as a single mother. At the time, Amanda was chasing her two-year-old daughter and leading writing workshops for single mothers in New York City. Lisa, who had also been a single mother, and juggled baby, graduate school, and a full-time job, had always worked with organizations promoting economic justice for women. She recognized the steep climb Amanda was about to face. Over the years that followed, we collaborated on research, sharing our thinking and writing, working toward making public the institutionalized inequities surrounding low-income mothers and children.

More important than our shared life experience and collaboration, we both understood that for us, through education and future earnings, the hardest times were temporary. What drew us to work together above all was a shared commitment to using the privileges of academia—research, writing, and public voice—to connect with other mothers who, without a national economic reckoning, would never climb out of working poverty. That is why we wrote this book.

GETTING ME CHEAP

1

Girls Step Up

Maya

"I was very good in school . . . then it all fell on me."

Maya, a thirty-one-year-old Latinx mother of two young children, was clearly proud of what a good student she had been throughout her high school years. "I was very engaged when I was in school. I did really, really good in school. So I was involved in everything, like the human relations club, the debate team. I stayed after school every day and did that on my own. I always was the one to take initiative and just sign my own self up. Like I did technology programs, I won trips to New York. So I was, like, really, really involved in school."

Maya was the oldest child in her family, with five younger brothers. Her father worked different jobs, nothing steady, "just, like, dead-end jobs, you know, like, here or there, you know, under-the-table jobs; my mom never worked." Her family relied on a mix of wages, formal and under the table, with some public assistance. Despite unstable family income, she managed to enjoy high school and excel. But then, "the way that my family got, it fell on me. My brothers were having it kind of rough."

At that point, Maya decided to focus all her energy on her siblings instead of her own future. Despite graduating with good grades, "I couldn't really further my education after that, because I kind of had to, like, take over things. And because I'm the oldest of six; I have five younger brothers that are . . . well, I'm thirty-one, my oldest brother's only twenty-five. So when I finished high school, he was still, you know, he was only twelve. And everyone else was a lot smaller. So since our parents, you know, at that time, really couldn't do a good job for us, I had to, like, step up."

Maya's story was unique in many ways and also so ordinary among girls growing up in a working poor family. We heard it many times. It is a script that runs across race, ethnicity, religion, geography, and country of birth. It is about children who step into adult roles because their parents do not earn enough to buy them a childhood. Family history and culture would tailor the nature of girls "stepping up." Women might reference racial identity, immigration experiences, and kin networks in how they were taught to help their family overcome waves of hardships. Some, like Maya, spoke of low-wage dads and of mothers who could not meet all the domestic and care demands that were invariably carried by women. Some spoke of single moms who worked two jobs and needed their kids to manage homelife, most often relying on daughters. A few described intergenerational and blended households in which there were younger cousins who needed care or grandmothers who had helped raise children but then needed care reciprocated. The accounts differed, but at the root of all of them it came down to poverty wages coupled with living in a society that has no commitment to protecting and nurturing children—

not unless their parents are affluent. These workers are paid poverty wages while their kids are, as one mom put it, "cast aside." In the United States, this is the common ground of low-income girlhood, yet it is all but absent in most equity and feminist narratives.

Maya clearly understood the impact of family demands in determining the next stage of her life. "So I really didn't get to do anything else after that, except go to work, you know, and kind of take care of things for me and my brothers. So, living at home and then you were just helping out at home and working. And then I had my oldest, when I was twenty-one, three years later, and we stayed on with my mom. And my younger brothers."

Looking back, Maya explained how she and her partner factored her family's needs into their decision-making. They were in a position to start an independent life with their new baby, but "we didn't feel like she [Maya's mother] was prepared to be on her own without someone, like, handling all the responsibilities. So we kind of put our lives on hold to maintain what my brothers had at the time, until we were able to kind of separate ties and, like, you know, move, move out and start off on our own without having to worry about her and them as much."

Maya spoke about a father who could not earn a higher income and a mother who had become overwhelmed by poverty and children's needs. For all of her enthusiasm and energy, Maya was caught and her life was held back. "My mom, like, she just didn't have, like, enough fight in her to really, like, overcome everything that was, like, what was going on. So she was, like . . . she just gave up in a sense, you know. I had to stay and do for my brothers; they probably would have ended up in the system, or, you know, would have ended up in a much more different path than what they did. But sticking around and investing in them the way that we did, that kind of did help, at least until they were old enough to be able to fend for themselves."

In an economy that wage-impoverishes parents, coupled with government policy that puts families at the bottom of national priorities, it is left to children to "stick around and invest" their youth and dreams. Girls' lives are a hidden cost of widespread low-wage jobs.

Bella: Work as a Family Affair

In 2016, white, working-class Bella described family demands that were very similar to what Maya faced. Lisa met Bella at a café in downtown Portland near the urban university Bella was attending. She brought along her five-year-old daughter, who pulled out paper and crayons. "She's used to waiting for me. She's patient," Bella remarked.

Bella grew up in the rural West near a town that's been losing jobs for years. Her family was always working hard and always poor. Her parents juggled seasonal farmwork and local service jobs that would ebb and flow with tourism, crops, and weather. Her parents would jump on a sudden job offer that could boost the family income by a few thousand dollars despite the disruption it would cause to the household. Bella described her parents' strength and hard work for family survival with obvious pride. But she pointed out that chasing wages meant her parents disappeared, sometimes for weeks;

Bella's father would be gone for even longer stretches. When the parents left, she and her siblings had to take over the house and farm "and not talk about it at school." Bella, now thirty-five, thinks that other children in her northwestern rural community "were in the same boat, but you just knew not to talk about it." One of the effects of this way of life was that no one was watching her schoolwork or attendance. When her mother called home, she would ask about school, but "really, we could say anything. What could she do?"

In Bella's opinion, her parents' relentless search for sufficient income contributed to their children's irregular school attendance and tendency to get caught up in "risky stuff." Eventually, Bella dropped out of high school. She earned a GED in her twenties and then, as a single mother of a five-year-old, pursued a college degree. But she believes that she was slowed down every step of the way by the weight of her family's needs. Like Bella and Maya, many of the women we interviewed marked early family demands as a dominant influence in determining their life course. But this working-class girl's life has captured much less attention than has the plight of higher-income, largely white girls whose well-documented struggles with self-esteem, body image, gender roles, and "agency" have dominated research on girls' "empowerment" and gender equity.

Research and policy attention to children's work in low-wage families is sparse. But what exists resonates with the stories told by Maya and Bella. Some studies have uncovered that these children are significant caregivers, spending some or much of their youth either caring for younger siblings or being cared for by older siblings. These early family responsibilities were recounted by many of the working poor moms we met. They reflect the phenomenon sometimes called "little mothers"—gendered care work that researchers describe as duties girls do with little reflection or resistance, regardless of the impact on their lives.[1] Research on immigrant children points to a keen sense of family obligation that, while demanding, is also a source of strength and identity. More than two decades ago, Abel Valenzuela examined children's resettlement responsibilities in families that had emigrated from Mexico.[2] He found that children take on considerable responsibility and that girls participate more than boys in tasks that require detailed explanations, such as translation for parents or advocacy for family needs. More recent research on adolescent care of younger siblings echoes this pattern. While older brothers might offer valued presence and playtime, adolescent girls provide the conventions of motherhood—physical and emotional caregiving—to younger siblings.

Genesis

"I have to keep in mind that I'm not her mom,
I'm her sister."

In a *New York Times* article, in November 2021, the journalists Eliza Shapiro and Gabriela Bhaskar introduced readers to Genesis, a sophomore in a northern Manhattan high school whose family was from the Dominican Republic.[3] Genesis was college focused, interested in architecture, and thinking about spreading her wings as she looked ahead. But the pandemic upended the family's rhythm. Over the six months documented by the journalists, Genesis not only had to transition to online learning for her junior year of high school, but she was responsible for overseeing her six-year-old sister Maia's schooling. Their single mother worked two jobs, so Genesis had to get her little sister up, fed, and onto the computer. "The rest of the day would be spent toggling between her own assignments and monitoring Maia's needs, which invariably won out." As the months passed, she spent hours each day trying to help her sister learn to read. As she described her role, Genesis said, "I have to keep in mind that I'm not her mom, I'm her sister." But she worried about how hard her mother struggles and, looking ahead, that it would be difficult to move away to college, far away from Maia and her hardworking mom.

With some ups and downs, Genesis made it through high school buoyed by friends, family, and determination. Importantly, *her* story got told. The attention that comes with a substantive *New York Times* article exposed a long-ignored truth about girls' lives in the United States. Yet the demands and capabilities revealed in young Genesis's daily life, while particular in detail and character, have been playing out throughout the nation for decades.

Unequal Girlhoods

Annette Lareau's research draws out and explores differences in parenting approaches that reflect class and race in the United States.[4] Children of the affluent are recipients of intensive parental attention, largely expressed through a wide array of enriching activities, counseling, sports, and other opportunities for individual cultivation. In sharp contrast, working-class children are expected to be self-sufficient and responsible for meeting basic milestones at school and in the world. Claire Cain Miller has reported on research that shows parents of all different income levels aspire to this intensive ideal, setting up low-income parents to fail since they don't have the time and resources to devote to endless carpools and activities.[5] Moms talked to us about the guilt they felt when forced to take low-wage jobs and patch together care for their kids, which often fell apart. They were frequently leaving children in "self-care" and relying on teens and children, predominantly girls, to take care of even younger children. Lisa recorded a teen girl who, upon listening to other girls describe their routine family-care work, said, "It's all true. It's all similar. I am the oldest daughter too . . . living with my mom and my three siblings, so I had to play my father's role, and I had to be the father. . . . And it was a big responsibility and it changed me a lot."

Wendy Luttrell points to the role of schools as reinforcing this classed framework.[6] She examines how schooling is organized around an "illusion of the 'care-free' student." Presumably, the 'care-free' parent is the female caregiver who is doing all the work behind the scenes. This model may in fact be the reality of wealthier children in the United States with some of the caregiving duties performed by hired help. But we heard how children face schooling expectations that largely ignore labor market pressures on their parents, pressures that configure family life beyond income poverty. Instability and uncertainty are absolutes for parents in millions of low-wage jobs. Freedom from daily care work and economic stress reflects the lives of affluent youth whose families can purchase all kinds of care and enrichment services, technology, and other options that free children to pursue self-cultivation. But for working-class and poor children, this kind of childhood is like another country, a far-off life. In the United States, childhood is a commodity reserved for those wealthy enough to buy it.

The contrast between growing up female in lower- and higher-income America emerges in many arenas. Dan Kindlon, a clinical psychologist and lecturer at the Harvard School of Public Health, described his revelations about today's "postfeminism" generation of young women, partly gleaned from coaching his daughter's softball team. As he describes it, unlike their mothers, girls take for granted equal rights and even outperform boys in terms of grades, honors, graduation rates, and college graduation. Kindlon explained to *Harvard Magazine* that as a result, these "alpha girls . . . are starting to make the psychological shift, the inner transformation, that Simone de Beauvoir predicted" in 1949. "'Sooner or later [women] will arrive at complete economic and social equality, which will bring about an inner metamorphosis.'"[7] What girls today are saying, adds Kindlon, is "I have flexibility that no other woman has ever had in history, or certainly not in any numbers, and I can play any role—'Bring it on.'"

This representation of girls' lives and their growing power resonates among largely white, higher-income families. But the girlhood we heard described is generally missing from popular campaigns for girls' empowerment, for building feminist pathways into STEM careers, and for nurturing girls' leadership skills. Many of the women who traced their biographies with us noted how deep family ties and brutal wage poverty were imprinted on them right from the start. The economy gets their moms' work for cheap and, behind that, children subsidize low wages by filling in for adults. Just as low-income women are overlooked in a personal choice model that dominates work and family debates, low-income girlhood remains missing from mainstream narratives about girls' lives.

Alania

"There was no one else."

In the summer of 2020, Lisa was gathering accounts about the challenges of running family childcare centers amid the COVID pandemic. Alania, an African American woman in her thirties, was describing complicated demands on childcare providers, remarking that it is hard work in the best of times and had become ten times harder in a pandemic. Then, in an aside, she mentioned that in her early twenties, she "decided to just quit my [medical technician] job and open up a childcare center because my brother was young, and he couldn't take care of his baby."

By 2020, she'd been working as a childcare provider for more than twelve years. "Actually, I have a medical technology background, that's my degree. I only got into childcare because of my nephew. He had leukemia, and he kept getting sick at daycares." Alania concluded that the only way to keep her fragile nephew safe was to be the one to watch over him.

"I quit my job and opened up [a home daycare] because my brother was young. I had adopted him when he was fourteen.

And you know, his child was going through a lot, and my brother was at a young age."

> Lisa: Wait, Alania, can we step back? So how old were you when you adopted your brother?

> Alania: I was nineteen years old. We lived in Wisconsin. I adopted him when he was fourteen and my sister, she was twelve.

> Lisa: You adopted both your brother and your sister?

> Alania: Yeah.

> Lisa: And you were nineteen years old?

> Alania: Yeah. There was no one else.

Alania's adoption of young family members turned out to be intergenerational. "I became a mama too—my brother had a baby when he was fifteen, so really I had a new baby. I went into childcare, you know, I converted over from the medical to childcare. I really liked the medical technology that I was doing. It might have worked out better, but I had these kids, my brother and sister and then my baby. It seemed like the only way to make it work."

When her nephew was diagnosed with leukemia, he was ten months old. "His mom at the time was sixteen. . . . He [Alania's brother] was still a child, with a baby who was injured and in the hospital. Every time he got injured, his hospital stays were very long. So, while I was in school, and finishing clinicals for becoming an ultrasound tech, I started doing a program for childcare as well. I was doing double courses to get everything done. I completed my ultrasound, and I worked in that field. But I also applied to open a daycare. I needed my nephew to be in a safe place. The daycare opened, finally, after I was trying to get the paperwork done for a year. Then, my nephew was only able to be there, like, four months before he passed. He was so little. But, you know, I'd done everything to start the daycare. That's where I was. I've been doing childcare ever since."

While Alania's particular experience growing up in a hard-pressed family stands out, it echoes other women's histories. Over the past decade, we listened to women map biographies of commitment to take care of people that started in girlhood. Like Alania's casual aside during the interview, sometimes we heard a throwaway mention about caring for a disabled grandparent every day after school or taking on earning or parenting duties when a father died too young. Girls would be called on to help out after parental job loss, sudden residential moves, or the arrival of relatives doubling up in the household. With all their singularity, these personal accounts reflect decades of statistical research on economic, educational, employment, and family disruptions that plague low-income family life. But there has been far less tracking of how the disruption of wage poverty spills onto children—and in particular onto girls.

The accounts share a common thread. Daily needs and chronic disruption in working poor families call up gendered demands that many girls feel they must meet. Low-wage parents, particularly single mothers, have limited tools to use to try to keep their families going. They might increase hours at their workplace or take on a second evening shift, which means being away from home even more. They might double up households, inevitably bringing more children into a small home space. They might add some off-the-books ways to earn additional cash. But any tactic they employed to provide more income was associated with a cost and usually that cost included more caregiving.

Keeping Families Intact: The Essential Work of Women and Girls

Before the pandemic, over 27 million children in the United States were living in low-income or poor households and many of those were working families: According to the National Center for Children in Poverty, more than half of low-income kids live with at least one parent who is working full time.[8] These parents labor in the nation's lowest-paid jobs, notably jobs primarily held by women who are starved for time, for work schedule regularity, and for decent wages. This labor market mirrors the life stories we gathered that reveal many mothers turn to children to help fill the gap caused by poverty wages. Mothers told us this was an inevitable pattern. When parents do not earn enough to buy the typical ingredients of a stable, safe, and protected childhood for their kids, they have to focus on ways to increase income or reduce the cost of going to work. For many mothers whose buying power has been losing ground over the last decade, the only option is to recruit others, often daughters, into family survival strategies. Listening to women chart their biographies, we heard this girlhood pattern described as ordinary, a simple matter of fact. It is a story about being young, poor, and female, often part of a family of color, and following a code that puts other vulnerable people first, just as Maya put her little brothers before personal aspirations and plans for her future.

Embedded in many of the oral histories that women shared was a powerful message about the value of keeping your family going. The need to recognize and prioritize this value is hardly a concern in higher-income families—not unless they experience an extreme disruption such as a bankruptcy or a parental health crisis that, in effect, plunges them into conditions that are similar to those of working poor families. But the daily habits of the affluent do not include relying on teens to help pay rent to avoid eviction. They do not include juggling teens' high school schedules or eliminating their extracurriculars so that, when parents must work mandatory overtime, toddlers are not left alone. They do not include relying on phone check-ins throughout the night when working additional hours to make rent and leaving children in self-care. Yet these are the strategies described as ordinary in low-income families. Commitment to holding family together is the priority when income poverty means families are continually at risk of breaking apart. This is not a sudden crisis for millions of working people—it is a way of life.

Women reflected on how, as children, they understood that "all hands on deck" included little hands. They also understood that as girls they were important contributors in their families' maintenance. Alania understood that she was the center of her siblings' homelife. Genesis knew that without her care of her little sister, their mother would lose the family income. Bella and her siblings knew that they must hide periods of parentlessness or there would be no family at all. We heard a description of girlhood in the United States that receives little notice even among child development specialists; it is only state child protection regulators who might pay attention to children's family work—to gather evidence of bad parenting. Moms who spoke with us said that, of course, families hide the demands put on children because, if exposed, all that will come is punishment.

We heard another hidden account of girls' work for their families. Women reflected on how living up to the family belief in kin loyalty and caregiving was deeply valued. With great diversity in their backgrounds, many women revealed how periods of hardship were mirrored by the depth of their kin ties. These ties were described as precious as well as heavy burdens. Those who had grown up working alongside their siblings to keep things afloat often remarked on close relationships that lasted a lifetime. The ties became intergenerational too, expanded through their kids and their kids' cousins. Many spoke of their extended working-class family, tribe, or racial/ethnic community as sustaining and protective in a society that denigrates Black, indigenous, and other people of color as well as immigrants, and that economically erodes white working poor families too. The meaning of family might stretch to a local or racial or ethnic community or to a religious or geographic identity. Members of these communities would step in when truly needed. Yet, of course, any web of kith and kin needs attention, and that is largely gendered work.

Early Self-Reliance

Working poor girls were raised knowing that they had to grow up fast. One mom put it simply. She believed sibling care work and involvement in a local community center meant that "My daughter is very responsible." She saw this as demanding but also character building. She and other mothers critiqued a culture of selfishness that is rooted in wealthy family attitudes. Instead, they talked about the value of early responsibilities for "house chores," conserving food, learning to fix things, and generally figuring out how to be self-reliant. Telling your older child or your niece that she had to mind a baby was not, as they described it, a big favor. It was expected. They contrasted this with the self-absorption and consumerism described as typical among wealthy white children.

A few moms expressed disgust with behavior of affluent kids they witnessed either through social media or through an extracurricular sport or educational program that brought poor and wealthy children together. These moms said that *they* expected a higher standard of morals and more respectful behavior from their children. We heard this described as the way of "the Black community" or what "people do for each other in Hispanic families" or as ethnic or tribal customs of behavior.

Among working poor white parents, this emerged largely when talking about neighbor-to-neighbor obligations, family chores, and responsibility toward grandparents. Across significant identity differences, this was a common ground of working poor families. Moms wanted children to learn that you give of yourself even if you don't particularly want to and even if you don't have much. They believed that their children's work on behalf of siblings and extended family members enriched them, taught them self-reliance, and contributed to their ethical development. We heard how children have to grow up fast in working poor families, and they rejected the narrative that this is irresponsible parenting. It was about living in a society that has institutionalized wage poverty, racism, single-mother hardship, and an antifamily welfare culture. Moms taught early self-reliance because that is family survival, and it is also something of which you can be proud.

It was common in our interviews for women to express pride in their early capabilities, independence, and courage—often explained as part of race or class identity. Black women linked their individual determination to a greater cause, as part of an intergenerational racial justice movement in the United States. A working-class identity that was tied to a particular workforce or labor union was associated with loyalty to kin and self-reliance among white women. Latinx women would sometimes reflect on the strength of their parents and grandparents, in awe that they had managed to make their way to the United States despite low wages and xenophobia. Danielle, a Puerto Rican mom from Connecticut, explained intergenerational care as the heart of her family. She helped to raise her siblings with her grandparents' help and said their influence shaped the person she's become. "My grandparents, my mother's parents, played a major role in our household growing up, and they kept us afloat most of the time, until I was able to go to work and start doing it. They instilled different qualities in me that I still have to this day, and they meant the world to me," Danielle said.

We heard about the value of keeping family intact, caring for kin and community, and about the strong, self-reliant women that can emerge. But alongside that, many women talked about demands on their time as children, the thwarting of their personal aspirations, and the heavy weight they always shouldered.

Nanette, 2019

Lisa and thirty-four-year-old Nanette, a Native American, met midmorning in an all-but-empty coffee bar north of Portland, Oregon. Nanette came with a four-year-old, Toby, one of two children she has been watching during the day while her own nine-year-old son is in school. Lisa brought coffee and a cup of hot chocolate to the table. Nanette reached out for Toby's cup to make sure it wasn't too hot. She told him to blow on the top carefully, so the whipped cream didn't fly off. "You don't want to lose *that*," she said to a grinning Toby.

Nanette took sips from her coffee and talked about her work caring for people.

"I worked all kinds of jobs. Like homecare, nursing homes, cleaning too. I look for jobs that I could work around my son, when he's asleep, or now, when he's in school. I'd started out taking care of my brothers. I was fourteen. So that kept going. Now, I take care of two kids in my home and I do home [elder] care. I just take them with me. She [her eldercare client] doesn't care, and I make sure no one sees them [the kids]."

Lisa: What would happen if someone saw them?

Nanette: You're not supposed to bring kids [to clients' homes as a licensed homecare worker], and if you are a certified daycare provider, you don't just take the kids to another job. I tell them [children's parents], so they know. You're not supposed to mix them. But I can't make my bills otherwise.

Neither of Nanette's jobs was full time, and even if they were, she would earn well below a sustainable income.

Toby spilled what was left of his hot chocolate, and Lisa and Nanette grabbed napkins to mop up. Nanette assured him it was nothing to worry about, but he looked so sad Lisa wanted to get him another cocoa. Nanette vetoed that, saying he'd had enough sugar; time now for a cup of water. Nanette took out toys, and Toby rolled a little truck on the table, rumbling engine sounds quietly.

Lisa: What's the most you've earned in a year?

Nanette: I don't really know exactly. Not enough. I think the most was maybe $28K but some is cash, it's not on the record. But, no, never enough to get by. I still sell plasma every month.

Lisa: Why did you start caring for your brothers that young?

Nanette: There wasn't anyone else. It was me, or they'd be alone. So, it was me. I started missing school and all that. But before, I wanted to be a marine biologist. I know that's hard to believe where I am now, but I did. I wanted to be a marine biologist.

An hour later Nanette left the café holding Toby's hand. She headed down the busy Portland street, off to pick up her son and then, later, to her eldercare job.

Inequality, Race, and Single Motherhood

Some of the women we interviewed directly blamed the labor market for eroding family stability. They spoke of parents' jobs in retail, care work, cleaning, hospitality, and food service that guaranteed the family would have unpredictable schedules and economic struggles. Erica, an African American single mom from Boston, was working toward her college degree in 2011. She said that in her family, multigenerational women kept them intact and moving up. Her grandmother was a domestic worker, and her mother was a nurse's aide. Erica said that "they were worked hard and paid shit," and Erica believes intergenerational Black women's wage poverty had a profound impact on their children and beyond. They don't get "the privileges that good money brings" that she observed among other young women, mostly white, in college. Erica, who had a baby in her senior year of high school, spoke about how her mother and grandmother made sure she graduated and pushed her to go to college. "They were, like, 'Uh-uh, you are not sitting around here; get up and get going.'" Their help with childcare and housing made it possible for her to move ahead, and she expressed deep gratitude at the time of the interview that she was close to completing her degree in accounting.

It was particularly clear that the largely hidden labor of girls to grandmothers was essential in families of color. This makes sense. Black and Latinx workers are far more likely than white workers to be paid poverty wages. In 2017, according to the Economic Policy Institute, roughly 19 percent of Latinx workers and 14 percent of Black workers were paid poverty wages compared to 8.6 percent of white workers.[9] Compounding this entrenched racial inequality, the National Women's Law Center reported in 2018 that two of three mothers in the lowest-paid workforce were the sole or primary breadwinners for their families, and among Black mothers, 84 percent were sole or primary breadwinners.

Important too, though often ignored, is the rate of single parenthood in the low-wage workforce. Low-income families in general and Black and Latinx families particularly have a high rate of single motherhood. About one in four children at any one time live with one parent, most with their mothers. But that doesn't fully capture the magnitude of sole parenting because over the course of childhood, more than one in five children born within a marriage will experience a parental breakup.[10] Estimates are that a third of all children, disproportionately children of color and children in low-income families, will spend part or all of their childhoods in single-parent families. Most of these are single-mother families that rely on low-wage jobs to survive. The decades-long institutionalization of poverty wages and decline of public assistance means these families are headed by working moms who cannot make ends meet and must find ways to increase wages or reduce costs of family life. One of the only ways to try to offset poverty incomes is to cut childhood short. Parents must call up children, in particular girls, to step into grown-up shoes.

Caring for Our Elders

Childcare and housework were the most common activities that women described as everyday chores girls were expected to perform in their "little mama" role. But another category of care work was responsibility for elderly family members who needed physical assistance, health coordination, and personal care. Renata had been a personal support worker since her adolescence, as well as a homecare and mental health support worker. She said, "I believe somewhere deep down in my life, with my grandmother and my mother, this was how it would be. I've always been attentive to seniors and elders. So I would say that I have been doing this certified for over twenty years, but I have taken care of elders all my life." Renata went on to say that, in her family—a multicultural group including Native, Mexican, and white working-class ancestors—you have an obligation to tend to older people who, in their turn, had tended to you or your parents. "It's part of our culture. I was trained to do this as a teenager. It became official, as a job [personal support and eldercare work]. But we were trained to do it," she said. When asked who Renata meant when she said "we," she replied, "I mean the girls in the family. I mean all the children in my family. Mexican people keep their elders with them, and so do Native people and people out in the country. A lot of the girls, more than boys, because it's just more natural. Girls have more patience," she responded.

Renata's view was repeated by other women who spoke of assisting or taking care of older kin. The most common were the grandmothers who had often been significant caregivers for years, helping out their sons or daughters with child raising. A few years after Danielle and her partner had moved into their own place, her grandparents needed around-the-clock care. They left their jobs and moved in, taking care of the house, managing her grandparents' bills, and making sure they took all of their medications and made it to medical appointments. "My fiancé would do all the yard work and I would do the housework. Of course, we didn't have to pay any bills or anything because we were taking care of them. We were living with them full time . . . my grandfather wouldn't listen to anyone . . . because he had dementia. He literally only listened to me." Danielle and her partner knew they were putting their other work opportunities on hold, but she saw it as a natural obligation.

Other mothers spoke about determination to keep their elders out of institutional care. Ellen, a white single mother of one child living in Boston in 2013, went to her grandmother's house to care for her three evenings a week, alternating with her sister. As much as she had to juggle on her own, Ellen said, "After all she'd been doing for us, we had to take care of her." Ellen held a very dim view of residential care for low-income elderly people because she had worked in several of these facilities. "They don't have enough staff. So [residents] get left alone. They aren't changed enough, and sometimes you walk in and the smell hits you."

Ellen talked about individual care workers who shouldn't be doing eldercare because they "don't have the patience or compassion you need." But most care workers, she said, were trying to do a good job. She thinks that the larger society doesn't care about old, frail, and disabled people, not unless there's real money to be made on them. She and her sister decided that, as time went on, their children too will be part of their grandmother's care system, despite the heavy demands on all of them.

Choices and Motherhood

Over the last few decades there has been considerable research into the impact of maternal employment on child development, prompted in large measure by the major increase of working mothers since World War II. In 1950, only about 18 percent of mothers in the United States were working outside the home. By the 1990s, that had jumped to 70 percent. Since then, rates have stagnated, seen largely as the result of the nation's lack of support for working parents. Yet this was a profound shift in the convention of white, middle-class family life. Child development researchers began to examine effects of growing up in "dual-career households" or with an employed mom, including the impact of long hours of childcare, effects on kids' behavior and schooling, and the advent of the overscheduled child syndrome. While research findings differ, the framing of work and family research was that mothers had chosen to enter the labor market rather than remain at home caring for their children.

This is a distortion of what many professional women see as their right to have a combined work and family life, just as men have long had. For men, having both is assumed, but for women, their "choice" is sacrificing one or the other. But worse, this "mothers' choice" model completely dismisses working poor mothers. The 2020 Census Bureau report *The Choices Working Mothers Make* names strategies women use, like choosing part-time work, taking unpaid leave time, or exiting work for periods to provide care for children.[11] This acknowledgment of the high price professional women pay to raise the nation's children renders working poor women invisible. If the mothers we met decided to reduce their hours or leave work, their lights would turn off, their heat would shut down, their children would go hungry, and in time they would be evicted and join the country's swelling homeless population. Most of the women we listened to had never reflected on the best choices to achieve work and family balance or even recognized their struggles as falling under this umbrella. Choice had nothing to do with it.

The debate about work and family conflict is located in middle-class or affluent lives. Affluent families routinely purchase labor in the form of au pairs, domestic services, childcare, counseling, tutoring, eldercare, and extracurricular and after-school programs. Orchestrating these pieces is demanding, but it allows both parents to continue to pursue their careers, generally increasing their incomes over time. Alternatively, another approach common in higher-income families is "buying back" time, with a parent reducing hours to part time or stepping back from a senior-level position that demands extra hours of work.

Most often, low-income mothers described having no access to the resources requisite to making such decisions. They were chronically time and income starved. In fact, many of the women we interviewed were themselves employed in the very jobs that provide services that stabilize, serve, and comfort affluent families. Some worked in eldercare, home health, and childcare services. Others worked in jobs that provide food, cleaning, landscaping, dog walking, product delivery, transportation, and any-hour-of-the-day retail services. The work that these working parents provide eases the stress of work and family life among higher-income families. It buys them time off and time to go to children's sporting or arts events.

It buys family time. It allows children the time, comfort, and self-cultivation of a childhood. Yet while the lower-income parents, mostly mothers and disproportionately women of color, are providing all of these critical supports, they may be leaving girls at home just to keep families intact.

Toxic Girls' Work

In some descriptions of growing up, women talked about how mothers sometimes just fall apart, like Maya's mom. Under the assaults of endless money and care burdens, some mothers gave up, overwhelmed by depression and sometimes addiction. Some suffered from significant health issues, arguably brought on by poverty and hard work. From children's perspectives, these moms had disappeared. When they did—across all the diverse families—there was a similar code. Just as girls were expected to step up to subsidize poverty pay and parental absence, daughters were often expected to step in and take over entirely. In some cases, dads were present and tried to cope, and there might be a grandmother or an aunt who jumped in. But most often it was girls, whether Black, white, Native, or Latinx, who were asked to focus their attention on the needs of a family on the brink of falling apart. Women who grew up in these conditions contrasted heavy burdens of poor girlhood with the loss of adults—particularly mothers. When moms are very sick, disabled, mentally ill, or addicted, the burdens on girls are not just heavy, they become toxic.

Decades of research has established that low-income people suffer disproportionately from heart disease, diabetes, cancer, obesity, and depression. The difference in average life expectancy between wealthy and low-income people in the United States is now fifteen years for men and ten for women. This wide health disparity is the result of deep economic inequality and systemic racism. Low-income neighborhoods with the least access to healthcare are also most likely to experience the worst of environmental harms. Black mothers are three to four times more likely to die from complications stemming from pregnancy or childbirth than white mothers.[12] Alongside these sobering numbers are those of all the children who lose parents or live with parents who have been profoundly compromised. In our conversations over the years, we heard about chronic illnesses, physical disabilities, and depression in families, and in some cases, parents' illnesses seemed to define entire childhoods.

Jonelle, a "mixed-race" thirty-two-year-old, said that where she grew up in the rural West, boys learn to "hunt and kill and girls learn to take care of everybody." At the same time, girls spend more hours being little grown-ups because they do the "inside work" that never ends, while boys head outdoors. But Jonelle took the gender analysis to a deeper place. In her view, the skills boys learn—of repairing, plumbing, wiring, roofing, servicing old cars, and working farms—can be converted into formal or informal apprenticeships. Though not easily or reliably pursued, brothers can follow pathways that may lead to an actual livelihood even without a college degree. Of course, Jonelle pointed to all kinds of pitfalls along the rural way, particularly drink, opioids, accidents, and turning to crime. But if you're a boy who manages to avoid those and you accumulate some of the gendered skills that are required, "you can make enough to raise a family." Jonelle viewed the constant care work required of girls as "enabling dependency" rather than teaching girls a trade that might help them get out. Caring for traumatized people was an outstanding force in her childhood. If you are surrounded by traumatized adults who don't even notice children—let alone protect them—the trauma passes on.

"On my mother's side . . . she was adopted. Her [biological] parents were very messed up. When my mom turned about twelve, she started drinking, and instantly she was an alcoholic . . . creating a life of trauma. She describes it as a switch being flipped, and she just was very focused on, you know, getting that alcohol. And then she had two kids. She was married by sixteen, and she had two kids by eighteen. The father of her first two children, which are my sisters, used to just beat her senselessly and would often threaten her life; he shot at my grandparents. She got away from him and met my dad, but he turned out to be a nightmare, even worse, and he would drink heavily. You have a lot of trauma from this stuff. My mother eventually got away from him too. Growing up with my mom's addiction, I was put in a place of taking care of other kids. I was a little tiny kid babysitting more tiny kids. I was watching toddlers, babies. I was always put in a position where I was to care for somebody, and I grew up with extremely strong codependency tendencies and caregiver tendencies. So what I didn't realize was that was who I started to become—a caretaker."

Jonelle's account uncovers how gender plays out in the most extreme conditions. She was very clear that boys don't get off easy either, referencing how some boys died from overdoses or became "predators" and ultimately went to jail. But she pointed to the ways that being a girl and thus deeply attuned to her mom's illness and responsible for "mothering" smaller children "sucked me in for a long time." Jonelle believes that she was raised to be "codependent, to be a caregiver" and to ignore the harm that she was experiencing and that led to "years of self-abuse."

Jonelle worked incredibly hard to overcome these patterns rooted in her girlhood and still uses what she learned from her upbringing to help others. She works in an agency that provides services to low-income and mostly single moms. It was a perfect role for her, helping young moms build their confidence and gain employment skills. She is renowned at her job. Reaching out to some of the women she coaches, we heard her name come up repeatedly, most often saying, "Jonelle won't let me give up." Jonelle has come to see her job as a way to funnel her caregiving talents, not to enable dependency but to transform poor women's lives. This is caregiving infused with power and purpose. "There's nothing they can say that I don't understand. I say, 'See what I overcame? You can do it and I will be there.'"

Keeping Girls' Work Hidden

Mothers are very cautious in sharing how they may be leaving children alone, or relying on older children to tend younger ones, or leaning on children emotionally when overwhelmed. During 2020, listening to mothers talk about surviving the pandemic, we heard reference to a ten-year-old tending to a four-year-old when a single mom was called in for ten-hour shifts at a nursing home. When trying to follow up on the story, we found that door shut. Several other mothers said that they couldn't take the risk of describing their child-minding arrangements. Beyond moms' feelings of guilt, they lived with the knowledge that child protective services is always in the wings and not as an ally. A 2017 *New York Times* op-ed by Emma Ketteringham, managing director of the family defense practice for the Bronx Defenders, described the child welfare system this way: "The problem is not that child services fails to remove enough children. It's that the agency has not been equipped to address the daily manifestations of economic and racial inequality. Instead, it is designed to treat structural failings as the personal flaws of low-income parents."[13] Mothers' fears are not unfounded; research has long shown that low-income, poor, and minority families are much more likely to face intervention by child protective services.

In early 2021, with lives turned inside out by the pandemic, we interviewed thirty-year-old Tam, who worked as an essential grocery store employee. She mentioned leaving her two young children home alone. At first, Tam said it would happen only occasionally, for half an hour or so, when her fiancé had to leave for his home delivery job, and she had to work overtime. But as Tam talked more, it became clear that her children's self-care covered more of the day, and sometimes on weekends too. The family daycare they had relied on before the pandemic had closed because the provider couldn't stay afloat and efforts to get help under the 2020 Cares Act had been unsuccessful.

Tam had two worries. One was that "child welfare will find out and they'll file on me." The other was that something might happen: a fire, a break-in, or one of the kids would get hurt. She actually called her union steward to ask if she could get in trouble for leaving a six-year-old in the care of her nine-year-old daughter. The answer was unclear. But Tam heard that, among co-workers, this was happening in lots of families. How much is very hard to say: parents know not to talk about this, to keep this kind of information quiet. But patterns of relying on children to care for younger children and oversee households, moms told us, were expanding out of pandemic necessity. We know this virus hit women the hardest, but behind them it was also clobbering girls.

Funneled into the Worst Jobs

Many of the women we interviewed who worked in low-wage retail, service, and care occupations traced a path that began in a working poor family and led to a no-future job. Drawing out offhand comments exposed how early gendered obligations funneled women into poverty work. With variations unique to every family, the overwhelming force diverting girls away from nurturing their own development was their parents' low wages. Poverty pay kept them from focusing on schooling, friendships, budding talents, extracurriculars, and, most of all, just focusing on themselves. Alania had originally pursued a career in medical technology before turning to childcare to protect the children in her family. Nanette had wanted to be a marine biologist but buried that dream because others needed all of her attention. Ambitious Maya put her academic goals on hold for her siblings, ultimately caring for little brothers and her own child, while standing by her fragile parents.

They had to forgo life dreams to help their working poor families and wound up being sucked into the vast low-wage labor market. It is a market hungry for workers that can be paid cheap, now hungrier than ever in pandemic recovery mode. Girls particularly subsidize parents' poverty wages by providing all kinds of domestic and care labor. In turn, many become the next generation of poverty-waged servers, care-givers, cleaners, and salesclerks providing comfort and convenience for others—but costing them everything.

2

Shifts to Work Any and All the Time

"You are so disposable, literally anybody can do your job."

Jill got her first job in the restaurant business in Connecticut when she was sixteen, but the lifestyle that goes with waiting tables became unsustainable after her daughter was born. A white mom with a four-year-old daughter, Jill described working from three in the afternoon until midnight or, if it was a double shift, from 10 a.m. until midnight. At the time, Jill and her daughter were living with her parents, who both worked full time but were home in the evenings to help with childcare. Otherwise, working in the restaurant business as a single parent would have been impossible.

"Your schedule can change at any time. You could be working seven doubles and making great money, but you are never home, right? Or then, the next week, something comes up or there is someone who asks for more hours who has been there longer, and they put you down for only three shifts, not even doubles. And you're, like, what the hell is this? It's never consistent hours, and nobody cares. Because you are so disposable, literally anybody can do your job," she said, explaining her decision to stop working in restaurants when her daughter was a toddler.

Next, Jill landed a position as an assistant to a real estate paralegal, which gave her a taste of office work. "That's what I want now," she said. "To be an executive assistant or something like that, helping out in an office with a regular schedule and all that." The gig working for the real estate paralegal, however, turned out to be short-lived. "She didn't understand the whole childcare thing. She wanted me to work around her schedule, but at the time I had this really cheap childcare, so I had to work around that."

Low Wages and Irregular Hours

"You never know your hours or how much you're going to make."

Retail, sales, food preparation, and restaurant jobs are known for having unpredictable schedules and low wages. Research by the Bureau of Labor Statistics and the Economic Policy Institute reveals these job sectors represent a huge chunk of the labor force in the United States.[1] In 2018, close to ten million workers were employed in retail sales as cashiers or frontline supervisors and roughly thirteen million were restaurant workers.[2] While both men and women are employed in these industries, women and Black and Latinx workers tend to be concentrated in the lowest-paid slots. Cashiers, at the bottom of retail and sales, earn a median hourly wage of $10.78, and in 2018, 75 percent of them were women.[3] In 2015, Catherine Ruetschlin and Dedrick Asante-Muhammad, researchers at the U.S. think tank Demos, found that retail employers paid seven out of ten Black and Latinx sales workers less than $15 per hour, while only 58 percent of white workers earned that little.[4] Workers in combined food preparation and service, including fast foods, earned a median hourly wage of $10.22, and this workforce was 62 percent female in 2019.[5] The average annual income for fast-food workers is only $13,500 per year and their average age is twenty-nine. Similarly, those working in retail are largely in their twenties and thirties, so many of these working women are also mothers to young children.

These labor markets, which employ millions of young parents, provide their workers with almost no paid time off—neither vacation, sick days, nor medical leave time. In part because of the low pay and lack of benefits, millions of food and retail workers rely on public assistance, such as SNAP (Supplemental Nutrition Assistance Program).[6] In 2020, the nonpartisan watchdog Government Accountability Office (GAO) revealed that roughly 70 percent of adults who receive Medicaid and food stamps (SNAP) are working full time. The research showed that Walmart and McDonald's were the top employers of benefit recipients, with Amazon, Kroger, and Dollar General also counting among their employees large numbers of workers who received SNAP or Medicaid benefits.

Lisa met Lenore, a thirty-two-year-old Black mother of two, at a community conversation in Denver, Colorado, in 2016. It was a Saturday evening and eight women sat around a table in an empty downtown office building. When we finished introducing ourselves, the conversation quickly turned to jobs and childcare. Lenore had moved to the city two years earlier because she had a sister living there. She was fleeing an abusive relationship, which was, as she put it, "hurting me but really harming my kids." Lenore's sister was a single mother of a twelve-year-old son and had a full-time job as a manager in a restaurant. Her sister was incredibly relieved that Lenore was finally leaving her husband, but Lenore knew she could not stay in her sister's small two-bedroom apartment permanently. As the discussion began, Lenore immediately focused on the impossibility of providing children with a decent life while she was working so much and earning so little.

Since moving to Denver, Lenore had started two part-time jobs: one in fast food and the other as a nighttime security guard. Still, she earned just under $25,000 a year. She received no job benefits and, in her opinion, "that's why they keep your hours low, so you can't get health [insurance]." She had no formal sick leave at either job.

Like most of the mothers we heard from, Lenore picked jobs that would allow her to care for her children. She went to work at McDonald's at 8:30 a.m., right after dropping her children off at school, and left work at 1:30 p.m. to pick them up. She would bring them home and spend the afternoon and evening overseeing play and homework and making dinner, until her sister returned from work with her son. Then Lenore would get on a bus to her second job as a security guard. She worked from 8:00 p.m. until midnight and occasionally on the week- ends. "I sleep from about 1:30 to 6:30 [in the morning]." Then she would get up to help the three kids get ready for school and do it all over again.

Lenore earned roughly $10 an hour for a total of about $450 a week. Half of her earnings went to rent, electricity, and heat, which she shared with her sister. Another week's earnings went to food (augmented by SNAP) and income-discounted transportation on city buses. She explained that after paying her share of the bills, she still had to cover her cell phone, the family's clothing, personal items, and all her children's needs for about $200 per month. That night, sitting around the conference table, Lenore told the group of mothers, "They want us to stay enslaved in these lousy jobs." She said the labor market is keeping working families so stressed by low wages they can never climb out of the hole they are in. Economists agree. The Economic Policy Institute's Family Budget Calculator gives an idea of the basic average costs of housing, childcare, health care, transportation, and groceries in specific locations around the country. We generated the chart here using the calculator to see what income Lenore would need to bring in, living in the Denver area, to support her two kids. She would need to earn an annual salary close to $90,000 to make ends meet. The women we met would have laughed at that figure. In fact, according to research conducted by Brookings, 53 million working people across the nation, 44 percent of all workers aged 18–64, earn an annual median income of $17,950.

Even when unemployment is low, researchers

ANNUAL COSTS	
1 adult and 2 children Denver/Aurora/ Lakewood metro area	
Housing	$17,016
Food	$7,215
Childcare	$20,179
Transportation	$11,760
Health Care	$7,762
Other Necessities	$9,776
Taxes	$15,825
Annual Total	**$89,533**

point out that many of the jobs at the bottom of the labor market are part time with low pay and too few hours to qualify for any benefits. Companies like Walmart, Target, and Whole Foods have been criticized for reducing employees' hours after small increases in wages. CNN reported that while Target pledged to raise wages, some workers claimed their hours had also been cut, keeping incomes flat.[7] Even when it's hard to see, there is corporate gain embedded in part-timing employees and growing the gig sector of the economy.

Juggling Multiple Jobs and Ever-Changing Schedules

"Just-in-time scheduling is a nightmare for mothers."

Often, parents like Lenore try to offset low wages by taking on multiple jobs and balancing irregular and seasonal work schedules. In hospitality, food, and retail sales, parents might not know their schedules until the day before work. In some jobs, they could be sent home after an hour or two if employers decide they are not needed. The hunt for childcare to match frequently changing schedules is all but futile; after-school or daycare arrangements could be obsolete and nonrefundable. Many retail and food service workers also have nonstandard work schedules, requiring workers to come in early, stay late, or cover weekends and holidays. Ella, a single mom in Portland, Oregon, described a typical day, juggling two jobs and three kids' schedules. At the time, she was working from 9 a.m. until 5 p.m. at a call center and from 6 p.m. until 10 p.m. at Pizza Hut.

Lisa: Can you describe a typical day, pre-COVID?

Ella: The call center would start at 9 a.m. I would have to get up around 6. Get everything ready, lunches and everything for the three and get ready. And then, I would leave my son and my daughter [at her parents' house]—they would keep them and drop my son at school. Sometimes they would let them sleep there, at my parents'. And then that way I would only have to worry about the baby. I would just take the baby to the babysitter and then leave her there for, like, almost all day long. From, you know, like, 7 or 7:30 a.m., because my commute was really long to the call center. I would say, like, from my house to the babysitter, I would say, like, thirty-five minutes. And then from there, just drop her off real quick and then, like, I would say twenty-five to thirty minutes to my first job.

Lisa: So, your workday with your commute, I mean how much, how much sleep were you getting?

Ella: Like, four or five hours; [laughing] I was so skinny at that time. I would, like, go running all day, grocery shopping and all that stuff—that's when I would take my kids with me and spend some time with them shopping.

Eventually, her frantic balancing act fell apart because the call center was sold to another company, and Ella lost that job. Unable to make ends meet working only at Pizza Hut, she applied to a pre-apprentice program, hoping to become an electrician and stop running.

Across her jobs, Ella had relatively stable hours, but often this is not the case. In fact, according to the women we spoke to, most employers wanted to maintain an open and flexible schedule to meet changing demand at minimal cost. Supervisors often asked mothers during the hiring process if they could be "available 24/7." Several women told us that "you have to agree or you don't get hired." We also heard about parents forced to leave young children on their own because they had to go to work early, stay late, or report to work whenever called. This "just-in-time scheduling" is a nightmare for mothers who are constantly patching together after-school and sick-childcare, homework oversight, school meetings, and the infinite variations of child raising while employed.

In the spring of 2019, a local aviation company hired Jill as an office assistant doing client services. "So I finally got one of these jobs where I could work from home or go into the office. I had a cool schedule too. I was working four days on, four days off, twelve-hour shifts. So I would have four days off in a row with my daughter. But I also love working that regular nine to five too, because then you get the whole weekend off," she said, clearly just craving the kind of predictable, regular schedule that you can plan around. Unfortunately, after only a few months, the company became part of a merger and downsized, cutting her department. Since she was so junior, Jill was laid off.

While nine-to-five schedules match up with school and childcare center schedules, today roughly four in ten kids under eighteen live in a household with a parent who works nontraditional hours. An Urban Institute study of nontraditional hours found these households were more likely to be low-income, single-parent-headed, and minority.[8] At the same time, 98 percent of daycare centers offer no evening hours and 94 percent no overnight options.[9] Centers may accommodate professional working parents whose work responsibilities spill over into the early evening, but they are not set up for the most nontraditional, irregular, and unpredictable work schedules that belong to parents at the bottom of the labor force.

Higher-income workers might be able to work online or telecommute, but most low-wage jobs require worker presence—cooking, cleaning, ringing up sales, or providing home- or childcare. This divide became even clearer under pandemic "stay at home" orders. More than 60 percent of workers with a bachelor's degree or higher reported being able to work from home compared to around 20 percent of workers without a college degree, according to a Pew Center poll.[10]

Even pre-pandemic, mothers across the country described the way hours that changed week-to-week made it difficult to maintain a stable family life. If they had two jobs, the chaos doubled. They were negotiating with immutable institutional and market demands without leverage, and their families suffered the consequences. Decisions about applying to jobs, seeking a better position at work, going back to school, or even developing personal relationships all pivoted around children's care and well-being.

Alongside the schedule instability, some working moms did not know how much they were going to earn each week. If sent home early from work one day, or if a schedule changed and hours were reduced, wages too became unstable and bills went unpaid. Employers had the freedom to calculate the number of food servers, nursing aides, or sales staff they needed according to busy vacation or shopping seasons, hour by hour, and they cut or increased hours accordingly. Will Romano, a former Amazon warehouse employee, wrote about the company's practice of encouraging warehouse workers to take "voluntary time off" in an article for the blog hosting site Medium.[11] According to Romano and other employees, Amazon supervisors often encouraged workers to take unpaid time off, giving them permission to leave less busy shifts early; and some workers reported feeling penalized when they refused. While it might be tempting to head home early to your couch and kids, many employees depend on the hours to make their bills and may have already booked childcare to cover the shift. Parents told us about daily calculations of whether to buy food or pay rent or skip a doctor appointment to avoid a co-pay. Millions of workers face this kind of volatility of schedule and earnings, but it is most common among the lowest-paid hourly workers.

Jobs Without Benefits

"I have never had a job with any benefits."

Not only did few of the parents we talked with have access to official sick days, but when they had to stay home to take care of themselves or their children, they ran into trouble at work. One mother in Massachusetts told the group about being fired after she notified her boss that her kids were sick and she needed time off. Another mother who worked in the fast-food industry told the group her daughter "woke up sick and had a fever." The moms agreed it was better to call in than to leave a sick child to go to work and handle customers' food. But when she told her supervisor, she was fired. One study by Restaurant Opportunities Center United found that nearly 90 percent of restaurant workers surveyed received no sick days.[12] "In a restaurant, they are, like, if you're sick, you're sick. If you break a bone, that's on you, you pay for it. There is nobody taking care of you. There is nobody paying you anything when you are sick. There is no sick time. There is no sick leave. There is no leave at all," said Jill of her years of restaurant employment.

You might expect that working for a large chain like Dunkin' (previously known as Dunkin' Donuts) would be different. But in reality, Dunkin' franchises 100 percent of its locations, so employee experiences vary widely. Danielle told Amanda she started working as a cashier at a Dunkin' when she was sixteen. "When I was seventeen, I actually got promoted to assistant manager, and was an assistant manager for about a year. And then I got my own store, and I was a store manager for about eight years," she recalls. Although they offered health insurance, she found it difficult to pay the roughly $100 a week they would take out of her paycheck to cover the employee contribution. "I was paying, like, $85 a week for insurance that isn't even good, but I guess it's because it's a smaller company—like, it can be a franchise that owns only eight Dunkin' Donuts, so if not as many people pay into the insurance, the rates are going to be high," she said. When asked about whether or not she had regular paid sick leave if she needed it, Danielle laughed. "Nope, they didn't offer any type of benefits like that whatsoever." In fact, as a manager, Danielle said if someone else called in sick, she'd have to go to work without notice and stay longer if there was a problem at the store or they needed to schedule a last-minute inspection. In the end, the hours became too difficult to navigate. "I had kids, and I was just away from home too much."

Luckily, Danielle connected with a customer who helped her get a job at a local Stop & Shop. "I jumped for it," she said, because she knew "Stop & Shop was a union job, so it would come with all the benefits." At first, though, Danielle could only get part-time hours. "Once you go full time there, the benefits increase dramatically versus a part timer," she said. So once she was offered a full-time position, she stayed for five years until, as we learned in chapter 1, her grandparents became ill. "We had to take care of my grandparents, because somebody had to, and it [her grandparents' house] was just too far from the store. An Uber was literally $30 one way to get to work. When our car broke down and I called, I was literally sitting there thinking it was going to cost me $60 to go to work for one day."

Without paid leave or flexibility at work, it's very hard to deal with family crises both small and big. And these crises are more likely to come up for moms carrying a heavy care burden. We spoke with dozens of mothers who reported being fired or having pay docked because they had to change their work schedules to care for family members. A young mom who worked in a warehouse outside Boston told us that she went home early one day because her son's caregiver called to ˅ he was sick. Right after that, her hours started to get cut ＼ When she asked why she in particular was losing hours, ＼ told, "You have a son." Her supervisors had not been ＼ was a mother of a young child when she was hired.

Now, she said, they acted like she had "lied to them" by not mentioning her child, and she was being punished.

In Atlanta, the moms we spoke to pointed out that as soon as their children entered group care settings, they got sick more often—observations supported by pediatric research. Typically, new childcare arrangements accompany starting a new job, which is a bad time for the kids to keep getting sick. Children who enter childcare as babies or toddlers have early exposure to germs and get sick more often than stay-at-home children. But some researchers, such as Sylvana M. Côté, PhD, an expert on childhood illnesses, points to the advantage of germ exposure in preschool. "I argue earlier is better to have infections because then kids do not miss school at a crucial time—when learning to read and write." Similarly, Gail Demmler-Harrison, MD, professor of pediatrics/infectious disease at Baylor College of Medicine, calls the findings "good news for working moms." She offers this advice to mothers who send their babies to daycare: "Hang in there. It may be rough when they are young, but when they get to elementary school, they will be immune to many of the infections."[13] This research, while potentially offering hope for the future, may not offer much consolation to a low-income mom who is currently juggling work and kids without sick leave. According to the Center for Law and Social Policy, among private industry workers, only 47 percent of the lowest-wage workers have sick leave compared to 90 percent of the highest-wage workers.[14]

Beyond the critical need for sick leave, 93 percent of low-wage workers have no access to paid family leave for seriously ill or injured family members, according to the Center for Law and Social Policy. In fact, some demographers connect the double burdens that women face, working and raising children, with declines in both fertility and women's advancement in employment. Once again, this high cost of motherhood is even steeper for poor women. Several moms mentioned being ill and still going to work to save their few sick days to care for their kids. But hoarding those few days was often not enough. In Georgia, a mom recounted her experience: "My boss told me, 'This is your job; you need to be here.' Well, I know my kids are my priority. Yeah, and I did get fired from that job too." She worked in the health care industry. Another mother remarked, "You'd think that they'd get it" in health care jobs, that people get sick and need care.

Sometimes the sick person is the mom. Mothers told us that they either go to work sick or lose their pay, or sometimes their jobs. We heard from women working in childcare, eldercare, food preparation and serving, and hospitality who routinely went to work sick. They learn to disguise or deny illness, to just "push through." In fact, the very jobs low-wage women disproportionately do—jobs of caring, serving, and attending to people—tend to be the most intimate, requiring close contact with people, which makes this survival strategy even more dangerous for the general public. In the fall of 2020, in Portland, Oregon, a homecare worker admitted to Lisa that she has, in the past, worked when she was ill. She has gone into private homes and to assisted living facilities with a fever, suppressed by Tylenol. But she raised the rhetorical question, "Would 'they' stay home and maybe lose their jobs, ability to buy food and pay rent, because they don't have sick days? My priority is my family." Moms talked about taking Tylenol every three hours and serving food, cleaning hotel rooms, tending to elderly residents in nursing homes, and caring for other people's children. They would deny or hide illness (including, in one case, pneumonia) in order to meet their own family's basic human needs.

Many of the individual descriptions that we heard gave voice to national trends. A 2016 report on a poll by the National Partnership for Women and Families revealed that 70 percent of women in the fast-food industry went to work despite illness, including coughing, sneezing, fever, diarrhea, or vomiting.[15] And in the midst of a pandemic, the dire consequences of having our babysitters, homecare workers, and Uber drivers going to work sick came into focus; surveys showed that positive public opinion about providing sick leave to all workers increased dramatically. But for decades, low-wage workers have weighed their scant options. The loss of two or three days of income may mean not paying for electricity or heat during a cold winter month.

Pregnancy and Childbirth

Childbearing presents a whole other set of challenges. While technically not an illness, pregnancy and lack of available leave around the birth of a child can also cause massive disruption at work and home. The mothers we heard from were even less likely to have any kind of parental leave than sick days. Gloria, a young Black mother living in Denver, recounted to a group of moms about the cascade of events others at the table seemed to recognize as commonplace. When she gave birth to her premature baby after an emergency C-section, she was fired, over the phone, while still in the hospital. She was not eligible for even unpaid leave, under Family and Medical leave Act (FMLA) rules. Nor could she have handled the economic impact of leave without pay. Then, shortly after surgery, due to the loss of her income, her housing was in jeopardy.

As we heard from dozens of mothers, homelessness is the worst nightmare hanging over them; many told us they would do anything not to be on the street with their children. Gloria, still recovering from surgery with a tiny infant, made what she saw as her best play to ensure the survival of her family. "All I could do was take all the medicines they gave me in the hospital and go out and sell them so that once my baby does come home, she'll have somewhere to go," she said. The other mothers listened, and we heard a common refrain: "You do whatever you have to" to keep kids safe. But everyone in that room knew how Gloria would be viewed by those who do not understand the world she lives in. If she were observed selling drugs for cash with a baby in the neonatal intensive care unit, she would be branded the worst of mothers.

The entrance of a new baby in any family can bring a mix of joy and hardship. Moms told us about the upheaval surrounding the birth of a child without maternity leave, income, or accommodations to ease the transition home. More than their own hardship, they focused on the emotional toll on the family. Cynthia, also in Denver, explained, "I had just had a brand-new baby and I was in the hospital stressed out. I was worried about everything. Crap that I couldn't fix. I ended up in the hospital with a three-day-old baby, worried about how I'm going to pay the rent."

Cynthia's experience is the norm for low-wage parents. The United States ranked thirtieth (out of thirty-three member nations of the Organization for Economic Cooperation and Development) in public spending on families, which includes paid parental leave. Bright spots in the private sector, however, show that progress is possible.[16] Parents working in socially advanced companies, such as Patagonia and Google, benefit from flexible, paid medical and family leave policies. At Patagonia, women get four months of paid parental leave and access to on-site childcare, and the company pays for a caregiver to accompany parents on business trips. But other corporations have class-stratified approaches. General Electric and McDonald's boast newly expanded family-friendly benefits like extended parental leave but only for salaried, corporate employees.[17] The division is even clear at Starbucks; while salaried parents qualify for either twelve or eighteen weeks of paid leave, full-time hourly workers get six weeks. In fact, consistently, examples of nascent progress exclude hourly workers who arguably need these benefits the most. According to data from the U.S. Bureau of Labor Statistics, one in three professionals have access to some paid parental leave; among low-wage workers, this rate drops to only 4 percent.[18]

Cynthia, Gloria, and many of the other working mothers we met did not even have access to unpaid FMLA benefits when they had a baby because in one way or another they were carved out. Either they were working on a grant, contract, or temporary basis; their hours had been kept under the eligibility bar; their employer had less than fifty employees; or they did not have enough months of service to merit FMLA protections according to the U.S. Department of Labor. But regardless of all those ways to exclude low-wage workers, moms pointed out that, for them, unpaid leave is no leave at all. While Danielle had access to some unpaid leave at Dunkin' through FMLA, she said, "You had to get it approved to go out on FMLA, and it was really hard, because you would literally have to save up to prepare to be out for those weeks," which is nearly impossible for families like hers living close to the margins. Lack of leave time coupled with the needs of their other children affected mothers' job decisions. Jamie, who worked in a grant-funded position in the school system, said, "Thank God I had my baby in the summer because I had to take maternity leave, but I didn't get paid nothing during that time."

Moms Push Back

The women we spoke with understood that failure to meet impossible demands at work and home would be chalked up to evidence of parental inadequacy. Mothers explained that, when they were late or sought schedule changes, some bosses understood the conflicts but many defaulted to old stereotypes—that low-wage, often minority moms are disorganized and unreliable. This theme came through all our conversations. The volatility of jobs would be attributed to mothers' inadequacies, not the labor market. Poor working moms talked about feeling "looked down on" and judged as irresponsible. Black mothers were particularly likely to call out and describe this kind of disrespect at work. They referred to it as "biased" or "racist" attitudes among employers and supervisors. But they also called it "mother discrimination." A Black mom in Massachusetts said, "They [employers/supervisors] have that attitude . . . they think you're making it up that your child's sick, like you are making up excuses." A white mother in the same

community group responded, "Like their kids never get sick?"
But somehow the supervisors see *that* differently, the group
concluded.

Many parents pushed back against unreasonable job
demands and inflexible supervisors in whatever ways they
could. They prioritized teacher conferences, pediatric appointments, or attending their children's sports events, knowing they
would lose money or get in trouble for taking time off. In some
cases, they lost their jobs. One mother in Denver said, "I am
not the worker they want because I am a mother." She stopped
trying to explain to her supervisors why she needed time for
her children. She just took the time off and dealt with the consequences. Samantha, a white single mom of three kids from
Pennsylvania, made a point of telling her supervisors about her
kids, so when they tried to schedule her for late afternoons and
evenings, she would explain, "Those times don't work for me
because after school the kids have all these activities, and then
you know I've got to get them to do their homework, eat dinner, brush their teeth, and all of that." These tasks, of course,
comprise the basics of what we think of as mothering.

For Others, Quitting Was the Only Option

Sandra worked at an Amazon warehouse during the overnight
shift because her days were spent picking up and dropping off
her three kids. It wasn't the physical labor or the overnight
hours that forced Sandra off the job at Amazon, though; it was
her supervisor's inflexible policy on cell phones. "They made
us lock our phones away," she said. "As soon as you come in.
My daughter is diabetic, anything can happen overnight, and

there was no way to get in touch with me or a supervisor. They, like, give you this 1-800 number, and it's impossible to even reach a real person." With her supervisor unwilling to offer an exception because of her daughter's illness, Sandra felt like she had no choice.

The parents we spoke with were especially sensitive when lack of flexibility or unreasonable demands at work had a direct impact on their kids. In Atlanta, Sherry described the guilt she felt because her daughter was getting punished for being chronically late to school. Sherry said, "My [overnight] job was over at 7:30 a.m., but they'd need to be at school at 7:30 a.m., so I'd have to sneak out a little bit early. But then the school would give my daughter detention for being late. . . . She's not a bad kid. She's waiting at the door [of their apartment] for me to get her to school." Several moms said they also felt judged by teachers and school administrators for not being more present at their children's school because they were at work. In Georgia, moms described pressure from kids' teachers and school and daycare administrators to be more engaged. Mothers in Denver spoke about this pressure as making "you feel like the shittiest parent alive." They talked about how teachers and school officials blamed them for any issues the children were having at school and at times seemed not to believe their "work excuses." Some of the mothers explained that these school officials just did not understand the reality of low-wage jobs and the kind of family life that is correlated with wage poverty. Maybe, some mothers in the group mused, "it's because they have paid sick days and vacation time," so it is hard for them to grasp the lack of choice or routine that is forced on low-wage workers.

Motherhood Discrimination at Work

"At work, you have to hide or lie about being a parent."

In Georgia, many women talked about the pervasive "discrimination" against mothers, which forced them to "hide or lie about" being parents in workplace settings. It was commonplace to deny or not mention having dependent children (particularly young ones) during interactions with potential and current work supervisors. One mother said she would not even disclose to co-workers that she had a child, while another said that she told an employer her children were living with a relative. Another mom explained to the group that when she interviewed for a job, she fabricated childcare arrangements because "you won't get hired or you'll get fired if they don't like your childcare."

A grandmother from Atlanta advised others to "plan for getting fired" because it is inevitable. Raising children, she counseled, you have to "expect the unexpected," which often means disruptions in daily routines, including work schedules. And bosses won't typically "have sympathy" about your child's needs. This community conversation in Atlanta, like so many others, turned into a discussion about "parent discrimination" at work. One mother, applying for a job at a warehouse, said she brought her baby with her because she had no place to leave him and did not want to miss out on the possibility of a job. She made it clear to the warehouse supervisor that she would arrange childcare once employed, but she thinks the image of her holding a baby ended any chance of being hired. A mother in Colorado summed it up: "If they know you have kids, they won't hire you." Always hide your children, we heard parents advise one another in different states across the country.

Just as we heard that child hiding often starts before you even have a job, we also learned it may start before a child is born. Several mothers explained that "you will be fired" if your employer knows you are pregnant. This was a moment, among others, when we went beyond quietly taking notes as a neutral researcher is trained to do. Listening to women talking about hiding pregnancies, one of the facilitators of a Georgia community conversation said, "You know there's a law against that, right? There's a Pregnancy Discrimination Act that protects women from losing their jobs just because they are pregnant." The response from the group was universal: "Those laws don't apply to us." Whatever it says in the statute, at the bottom of the labor market there is little or no enforcement of women's rights. Until there is, poor working mothers told us that they use whatever tactics work. One mom in Atlanta said, "You have to work. You have to take care of these kids. You have to balance everything. You have to feed your kids."

How Can I Move Up in This Job?

To many of the moms, it was clear that in order to stop relying on help from the state or friends and family, they needed a path up at work. Jill said, "If I can't advance myself, how am I going to be self-sufficient ever? I'm looking at these jobs that start you at like $14 an hour, and I'm, like, 'I'd be making more money sitting at home collecting from the government than trying to get a job with you.' You know, I was making, like, let's say twenty an hour before, and there is no way I can make less than that with my daughter and my bills . . . unless you tell me I can start there, and then every six months or so we can talk about a little more, because for a while we can sacrifice things, like gymnastics for a year or whatever, so that I could have a steady job, then that's fine, we can do that, but so many of these jobs are just going nowhere," Jill explained. Recently, in a job interview, Jill asked about the possibility of promotion and was told directly there was no room to grow because they were a small company. "I'm thinking, 'Then you are not going to get somebody who has a family to take your job.'"

Over the years, we heard a few stories of supervisors who helped moms to move up. "I had a mentor when I started at Dunkin' who saw the potential I had, and so he invested in me. I became a store manager. But then he got tired of the company and decided to open his own restaurant. It was like night and day when this new manager came in," said Danielle. Without a real path up, moms' success becomes dependent on the continued availability of the person helping them. "Because the new manager didn't know what he was doing, certain months I couldn't make my goals, and so I wouldn't get my bonus." He refused to take her input about food ordering and costs, and the store started to fall short of its goals. "I counted on those bonuses," said Danielle. "I needed that $600 check per month on top of what my salary was already, because, you know, we needed that extra money." Between the demanding schedule and now a reduction in take-home pay, Danielle left Dunkin' after a few months under the new management.

Many of the moms said a supervisor could make all the

difference. While some might block their progress, others would look the other way, or refrain from docking pay or writing someone up for staying home with a sick child—small acts of kindness and understanding. Marcie, a white mother, was attending college in Oregon in 2016 while raising a young child and working at a pub in the evenings. She told us about her boss, Letitia, who tried to help her out. Letitia, a grandmother who had been a single mom two decades earlier, allowed Marcie to bring her daughter into a back room at the pub when the preschooler was ill and couldn't be left in the care of their young babysitter. Marcie came to work with blankets and Tylenol, and she could constantly check on her daughter. Marcie said she "got through that semester" because of Letitia's under-the-radar flexibility. But she knew that Letitia was taking a risk, hiding her compassionate treatment from the pub owners.

Paula, a Latinx mother of three living in the suburbs of Connecticut, spent close to a decade moving between low-wage jobs in service and retail before she found an "understanding boss" at Panera who checked in with employees to see who was interested in future management opportunities. Since her kids were still young at nine, eleven, and fourteen, Paula wasn't ready to move up yet, because of the more demanding schedule required of managers. Amanda talked to Paula in 2019, but they first met years earlier at the Panera where Amanda often came with her computer to write and where Paula worked as a cashier. One day, Amanda noticed Paula setting up her kids at a table in the back of the café. It was lunchtime on a weekday, and they had books, snacks, and electronic devices to stay busy. "If the kids have a day off school or something, I can set them up in the café with schoolwork or whatever—for eight hours if I need to," she said.

It took Paula nearly a decade to find a job where this arrangement was possible. Yet whether this flexibility comes from company policy or just her "understanding boss" Paula isn't sure—and doesn't want to ask. For now, she is just relieved to have a stable routine and some understanding at work that raising children is not always convenient or even predictable. But if that changes because a new boss is hard-line or they try to shift her schedule or any other of dozens of disruptions, Paula will start churning jobs again, keeping her kids in the center.

Before finding work at Panera, Paula spent seven years at McDonald's, at the same restaurant where the father of her younger children worked because it was easy to coordinate schedules. But eventually she quit, sick of being passed over for promotions, in her view because she was a mother. "It seemed like there would be opportunities to move up, but then I got beat out by a woman who had only been working there for, like, six months when I had been there for four years. She didn't have kids, and it just made her more desirable to them, I think."

Most of the women we spoke with saw little possibility of finding a better job with higher earnings. They dismissed platitudes about moving up through hard work and said their jobs had no or very limited career ladders. National research tracking economic advancement of low-wage workers affirms their experience. An article in the *Atlantic*, "Poor at 20, Poor for Life," summarizes research by Michael D. Carr and Emily E. Wiemers, two economists at the University of Massachusetts.[19] Their findings showed that over the last few decades, there has been very little mobility among workers with few chances to move up the income ladder; the only real change has been at the very top. In fact, researchers from the Federal Reserve point out that low-wage workers are "more likely to become unemployed than to move up the job ladder."[20]

Some of the moms went beyond their personal stories and critiqued the larger society. They rejected myths about pulling yourself up by your bootstraps, pushed back on narratives about Black women being "welfare mothers," and defended single mothers accused of having "that attitude," which all understood to mean irresponsible. These working moms saw through the rhetoric on the news and in public conversation that conjured racist stereotypes of irresponsibility and dependency. The unspoken message running through these discussions is that poor mothers—often single, Black, Brown, or immigrant women—deserve no better. They are not reliable workers; they are disorganized mothers who don't have stable arrangements for their children and are without a work ethic that prioritizes jobs. The advice that the Boston grandmother offered should be understood as self-protection: "Keep your business to yourself," she told the younger women. "Stay quiet and stay hidden. Truths about children, pregnancy, sickness, and family life will just be used against you."

We did not meet a single mother in our interviews or community conversations over the years who had moved out of the low-wage labor market without more educational attainment, certification, or job training. Yet the pathway to attaining higher education is also packed with obstacles. Paula started working at seventeen and never had the chance to attend college, but like many of the moms in these pages, she is determined that her children will get that chance. "My kids see me living this way, you know? I don't want them to run around paycheck to paycheck, like me. I want them to get an education so that it doesn't happen to them," she told us. "That's the most important thing."

Amanda reached back out to Paula after finding a COVID closure sign on the door of her local Panera restaurant in 2020. Paula said she was receiving unemployment, hoping the restaurant would reopen whenever things "go back to normal." Not working allowed her to be home with the kids during the shutdown, but that was hard too. "This distance learning is rough. Two of my kids failed because they didn't want to be on the computer," she said. Just like that, Paula's stable yet flexible employment and college dreams for her kids were suddenly in jeopardy.

3

Care Work for Cheap

"If you lose that job, it's going to be really tough to find another family."

In the spring of 2021, Amanda talked to Serena on the phone while Serena commuted home from her nanny job. Every weekday, Serena drives an hour from working-class central Connecticut, losing out on time with her own children, because affluent families pay more than she could earn closer to home. She works in a part of the state known as the Gold Coast, along the Eastern Seaboard, where the average home price is around $700,000 and median family incomes are among the highest in the nation. Here, she makes $25 an hour. Despite that wage, Serena says "you know, you . . . you're never gonna make more money than that," because the work she is doing has no ladder to better employment. Right away, Serena warned Amanda that she might get upset, talking about leaving her premature baby at home just days after discharge from the hospital to go watch other people's kids. She had been "counting on every single penny that I was gonna make up to that day," the day she was supposed to give birth. But Serena's third child came two months early, and because of the pandemic, "it's so hard to find a job," so she went back to work right away.

Because her hours can be cut on a whim, Serena always tries to work for two families. "When you just have one family that you are working full-time for, you don't have that security, because if you lose that job, it's going to be really tough to find another family that is going to offer you, like, forty or fifty hours per week, you know?" Casual replacement is the ultimate insecurity facing care workers employed privately by wealthy families. They may be relied on for many years to care for children, elders, or disabled family members and tend to a whole household. But when children grow older and elderly members die or if a family moves or decides to simply dismiss you, there is no pension, seniority, or social mobility gained. You start all over.

When workplaces shut down in 2020, one of Serena's families "paid me for one week, but after that, they were working from home, so they didn't need me, and that was it." After Serena's other family "found out that I was pregnant, they were really upset. And you know, they immediately tried to look for another nanny. And I told them that, listen, like, I'm gonna have my mom watch my baby so you don't have to worry about, you know, me being away for too long." Serena pleaded with the parents. But then the baby came early, and they wound up replacing her anyway. "I am the one that needs the job and there are so many people that will take the job. I need that money. I would have been willing to work for them for less money if they would have kept me, because, you know, I was already used to the routine and everything. But no, I was replaceable." Thankfully, Serena found a new family. But she decided not to tell them about just having a baby; she couldn't risk losing this job.

Serena came to the United States from Ecuador with her parents when she was nine years old. Without legal status, her mother had few job choices. She cleaned houses for wealthy families and got paid under the table. Often, she took Serena with her to wait in the car, and if the families were not home, she would help her mom clean. Like many of the "girls" in chapter 1, Serena was funneled into a particular labor market long before she grew up. By the time she turned fifteen, some of the families started asking her to babysit. It was a chance to make a little money of her own.

Unlike her parents, Serena had the opportunity to become a citizen and went to college to study psychology. "So I went to college and everything, but it didn't really work out financially, and my parents didn't really know how to help me. So then I went to a hairdressing school, and I was diagnosed with rheumatoid arthritis. I wasn't able to finish that either. So the only thing that I have really been able to support myself doing has been babysitting." By the time she talked with Amanda, Serena had been working as a nanny for over a decade.

Poverty Wages Without Benefits

There are millions of women working in care and domestic jobs whose wages are so low that even working full time they live in poverty. According to the Bureau of Labor Statistics (BLS), there are between seven and eight million workers in various personal and domestic care jobs in private homes as well as in care facilities. This employment sector includes personal care attendants, home health aides, nursing assistants, nannies and other childcare workers, and domestic cleaners. More than 90 percent of these workers are women and over half are Black, Latinx, or Asian American/Pacific Islander. According to a 2021 report by the Paraprofessional Healthcare Institute (PHI), a leading research institute on the health care workforce, these jobs are characterized by low wages, inconsistent hours, few legal protections, and little access to benefits or advancement opportunities.[1] Domestic workers are paid an average of $12.01 per hour, earning only about 75 percent of what others make in demographically similar workforces, according to the Economic Policy Institute.[2] It is not surprising that domestic workers are three times more likely to be living in poverty than other workers. Experts studying the domestic labor market consider the official numbers to significantly undercount this workforce since many domestic workers, like Serena's mother, work off the books.

Beyond very low wages, these jobs provide few, if any, job benefits, which may be offered or taken away at the whim of private employers. In 2020, the Economic Policy Institute noted that fewer than one in ten domestic workers have an employer-provided retirement plan and 80 percent get no health insurance coverage through their jobs. In fact, nine out of ten domestic workers have no paid time off at all—no sick leave, no maternity leave, no vacation, and no paid holidays. They also have very little control of their work schedules because scheduling is determined entirely by client needs. For example, Estelle, a homecare worker in Oregon, talked about how her families might go away for a week or two, without any prearrangement, and leave her income dramatically reduced. She said this happens to care workers all the time. Additionally, given that many homecare clients are elderly or live with chronic disabilities, they frequently require inpatient care instead of at-home care. Estelle remarked that with other jobs, like a nurse in hospital or a sanitation worker for the city, you still get paid even if the number of patients or volume of trash goes down temporarily. But in domestic and care jobs, all that risk is carried by the lowest-paid workers.

Serena has never had a nanny job with any benefits like sick or vacation days, health insurance, or parental leave. She laughed when asked if she had health insurance through her job. "No, never, but if they did [offer it], I think I would take that job, just because of that." Some of the families are more generous, she said, and maybe would pay her for a holiday, but with most of them this is not the case. "If that [holiday] falls on a day that you were supposed to work, you're not getting paid that day," she said. "With most of these families, they are paying you under the table. . . . None of those benefits really applies to you, and what can you do about it? You know, I am the one who really needs the job, and so I am willing to take whatever they throw at me."

Joan, a Black homecare worker in Massachusetts who assists disabled people, shares Serena's experience. "Even before COVID, I mean, a person that's not well doesn't care about whether it's Christmas or your birthday or Father's Day, Mother's Day, Easter, Thanksgiving. You just still have to show up, you know that's essential. I always worked holidays, always, always New Year's. It doesn't matter if you have to take care of someone. Yeah, there's no such thing as a holiday in my life."

Women who provide group childcare in their own homes

represent another part of the care work sector. Like nannies, domestics, and homecare workers, they earn low wages and most go without benefits or paid time off. However, these care workers, almost entirely women, often do this kind of work because it allows them to "work from home" and combine some earnings with mothering. Too often, though, family childcare providers inherit the instability of working poor parents who see their hours rise and fall, shifts dropped or added, often with little or no notice. Home-based childcare is used primarily by low-income families since it is less expensive than center-based care and, importantly, is more likely to be flexible for parents with nontraditional schedules. The growing popularity of an "open schedule" among low-wage workers spills onto the childcare workforce too. Providers point out there's a real disincentive to provide childcare for these families, another ripple effect of such bad jobs.

Going Above and Beyond for $25,000/Year

"You can't live on this."

Ramona, forty-eight, a white homecare worker in Oregon, described her exhausting overnight shift for which she earns $11 per hour. Her daughter, Carey, sometimes accompanies her, and so they split the wage. "The lady I take care of [Helena], since she's got dementia or Alzheimer's disease, she's like a toddler. Sometimes she gets erratic sleep behaviors and sometimes she can sleep good, and sometimes she gets picky about what she eats or she doesn't want to eat. And so then, I mean, it's your duty to make sure they're safe, and to be there and to look out for them. And so she chooses to move into the living room to sleep. So when my daughter and I go out there, we sleep in the living room because she's up all night. We can [lie] there and act like we're sleeping so that she doesn't want to talk. If she wants to get mad or if she catnaps, then we know at the time. . . . The biological clock is so different that they're up all night or whatever and it's your job to make sure they're safe, and before, she'd want to wander around in the dark outside or go up to the main highway, and it's a big crisis, because if she gets hit or the railroad tracks are there . . ."

Helena's family—two daughters and a son and their children—appreciates Ramona's coverage of the exhausting overnights. They see Carey as a second trusted person to alternate shifts. But none of the family members has offered to pay extra for a second person. Carey helps her mother on the exhausting overnights out of a sense of loyalty and concern for her mother's health. Carey's loyalty is valuable not only to Ramona but also to Helena's family. Ramona would likely quit without her daughter's uncompensated help. Like earlier accounts of daughters substituting for their mothers who were away from home working, growing and adult daughters, like Carey, may accompany mothers to clean, cook, and provide care. The result is an invisible wage subsidy, paid by low-income family members, to the advantage of the more affluent.

The low wages of personal and health aides are not always paid by families or individuals. Hilda, a white personal support worker for mentally disabled clients, earns about $12 an hour based on the wage level established by the state. The clients that Hilda serves are themselves low-income, and neither they nor the state system are set up to compensate her for the extra support work she does. Nevertheless, the health care and social services she provides reduce costs to the public by thousands of dollars. "You generally don't work with too many elderly, you generally work with people who are say, mainly age thirty and under, but it's definitely anybody who is, like, autistic, has mental problems, and you help them, support them throughout the day." Hilda says a lot of the work she does flies under the radar. She not only has to understand the often complicated health and social barriers facing her client and his family, but she also needs to assess where he can fit into a job and get engaged in the community to break out of isolation. She looks ahead for obstacles and helps prepare him.

Hilda also described caring for a woman with a colostomy bag that was ill-fitting because she had lost so much weight. "I mean, it was just dripping out, I'm just like, oh my God. The smell. And the thing is that we should have resources. . . ." Convinced that this woman's life was being steadily diminished, Hilda reached out to an acquaintance who was a doctor. "I was able to get her help. I was able to advocate for [her client]."

Hilda explained the steps she took: "I had a notebook and I wrote everything down. I did just exactly what [the doctor] said, and I called the insurance company the next day. I told them that I am going to be recording it, typing it, and giving it to every doctor that my client has, including her podiatrist, so this information is going in all her medical records, and everybody would be able to find it. That was number one. And number two, I had the right vocabulary. And let me tell you, the next day, she got everything she needed. Because these doctors work with insurance companies, and they know the right terminology; the insurance company's not going to tell you what to say to them to get the product. They're trying to give your client the cheapest thing, whatever is in their warehouse." When asked what would have happened to this client had Hilda not intervened this aggressively, she said, "Well, my [doctor] friend said she probably would have ended up in the emergency room or died." Hilda, a low-wage worker, did all of this lifesaving advocacy work after hours.

This kind of extra, unpaid work is also regularly expected of childcare workers. Celia, a white mother of two kids in Oregon, runs a preschool out of her home. When asked how long her typical day was, Celia responded, "I haven't counted it exactly but maybe twelve hours, usually about that." Celia described her routine: "My day starts, like, at 6 a.m., because there are certain things that I always do every morning before people show up. You know, like, make sure everything is right. I have to clean up different spaces, and I'd have to get the laundry out of the dryer and bring it upstairs. Make sure it's ready to unlock the doors, you know, turn on some lights, turn on the heater, you know, all that kind of stuff. Make sure food is defrosting that I needed out of the freezer for that day or, you know, all those little tiny things, that's on me. Typically, my employee would show up at 8 a.m. She would be taking care of morning duties. I would be unloading the dishwasher and making breakfast upstairs, and then of course managing my own children and whatever. Yeah, they were needing their mom, you know, making sure my oldest son had breakfast and we'll get ready for school and make his lunch and get his backpack ready—you know, before he had to go to school, and simultaneously being downstairs and managing parents dropping off, maybe needing to talk to me, cooking breakfast for eight kids."

Juggling numerous parents, getting one son onto the bus while the other one joins the kids at her school, getting food on the table, and setting up activities for that day: "It's a lot. Sometimes by 10 a.m., when they're all set and busy and fed, I am, like, 'Okay, I've done a day's work,'" she said. Hiring a full-time staff person helped, but paying her wages takes a big chunk out of the family's modest income. And even with that help, Celia keeps working hours after the kids leave to organize the next day. The children are picked up by 6 p.m. Then, "I hand my baby over to his dad who's home by then, and do another load of dishes, clean, sanitize [with COVID], make sure all my supplies are ready." On top of all that, since she accepts state subsidies, she has "tons of paperwork" to meet all the requirements. Celia does her paperwork and, if needed, makes parent calls before bed.

Celia is not alone among home childcare providers who struggle to provide childcare for lower-income families. The nation's minimum wage is so low, millions of working families are eligible for state childcare subsidies, but these subsidies come with regulatory baggage. To receive payment, a childcare provider must navigate state requirements and meet certification regulations. Should the particular state require that parents pay a high "co-payment" or their proportion of the cost, they often fall short. Or should family income suddenly increase with mandatory overtime or extra hours, their subsidy may drop off or the co-pay may rise significantly. A provider in Oregon, Diana, simply stopped taking any "state kids" because of the obstacles she faced. That state requires high co-payments and she said that parents, often single moms, would fall behind. Then Diana would see her own small weekly earnings shrink, and she would face the decision to "kick the family out." Diana said, "I tried to work with the parents, if they [were] behind, like set up a catch-up plan. But how could they catch up?" She also had to manage paperwork for the state agency dispensing subsidies, which required certain standards and reporting about her operation. It just wasn't worth it.

Caring for the Wealthy

Part of the reason Serena commutes so far to care for children in wealthy families is the higher wages. For Serena, seeing such wealth made it hard for her to understand when families tried to add on to her duties or save money in other ways. She recalled how her workload would gradually creep up. First, she says, they might ask about light housekeeping or, "'Do you mind cleaning the bathroom, in between watching the kids for a few minutes?' And then you are doing all this cleaning to save them a hundred dollars a month from having the housekeeper come." Serena had taken a job working for a family with three kids and low pay, because she really needed the money. But once the pandemic hit, they didn't want too many people coming into the house, so suddenly, "I was supposed to be the housekeeper, the babysitter, and the teacher." Serena explained her stress over the expansion of her childcare duties, since the kids were now home all the time and needing much more care and attention (and making more of a mess). The parents said they could not afford to pay any more because they "didn't know what was going to happen with the pandemic." But Serena knew what they were paying her was not affecting their lifestyle. "Yes, I mean these families have six- and seven-bedroom homes and they can't pay you this much more an hour?"

Nannies, housekeepers, and homecare workers are seldom in a position to renegotiate their wages even as employers expand or change work expectations. In fact, when employers ask for more help, it is hard to turn them down; saying no to a domestic employer can feel like a threat to a personal relationship. But the burden of this kind of employer-employee personal relationship is one-sided. Many domestic workers described when the employing family had a change such as a job change, marital separation, reduction of parent hours of work, pandemic, or other major shift, the relationship quickly reverted to the boss-employee dynamic. Abruptly, with a reduced labor demand, the care worker was no longer viewed as almost-kin; she is no longer "part of the family."

Beyond Poverty Wages, a Culture of Exploitation

We listened to domestic and care workers describe a job stuck in deep inequality and a culture of exploitation. These working moms, many of them immigrants and women of color, spoke about the ways they are constantly reminded that they are at the bottom of a class system. Beyond poor pay, they were expected to meet employers' changing needs, always subordinating their own. What's more, they were expected to authentically empathize with their employers' families while also accepting that their own children and families would be consistently ignored. As bad as the unpredictable job schedules of service and retail workers are, the job of paid caring takes on the burden of *mother work* that has no boundaries. Start and stop times were often ignored.

For mothers, this culture of exploitation particularly emerged in caring for the children of wealthy families. They would often encounter a stark division between "their kids" and "my kids." Amanda asked Serena if her employers ever invited her to bring her kids to work, especially if they were the same ages as the kids she was watching. Serena recalled only one instance. "There was a family I worked for and the mom would tell me, like, okay, you know, my son doesn't have a playdate today so you can bring, you know, one of your daughters, if you like. But it was one of them. I couldn't bring both of them." The employer was willing to have "one of them" to provide a play distraction for her own child. Yet she clearly felt no responsibility to consider the feelings of the children in the other family. Serena would need to select which of her children got to go and which would be left home, without a companion—"I kind of felt bad leaving just one."

Most families, including the ones she is currently working for, do not allow her to bring her kids to work. "I do wonder sometimes," Serena says, "like, why is that? I think they are nervous and maybe they wonder, like, what would happen if my kid was to get hurt?" That exclusion was common among domestic and care workers we met. A mom in Massachusetts, who provided cleaning and childcare to a dual-physician family, could not bring her child to the house, because "they thought it would take away from how I took care of their kids after school. Even though I'd known them since they were babies, and they knew how much I loved them." That the domestic worker's children might need their mother was never a consideration.

Serena knew she had to leave one of her nanny jobs when she realized that she was always coming home exhausted and in a bad mood. "I didn't even want to deal with my own kids. Usually when I come home from work, I have two hours to see my own kids, put them to bed, feed them dinner, read them a book, and go to sleep. But I got to the point where I was just picking up, like, McDonald's . . . putting them to sleep right away. And it was not fair to them. I was too overwhelmed. There was too much work, and I didn't want to put my kids through that." Serena began to view her care work for other children, affluent children from well-resourced families, as siphoning off mothering from her own children.

Work Without Boundaries

"Can you stay a little longer?"

Across the states where we talked to mothers, domestic workers described how the nature of their work makes it easy to exploit them. "Living in" puts them in the most vulnerable position of all. Before she had kids of her own, Serena held a few live-in positions to save on rent—but saw serious downsides. "There's no privacy because, obviously, you know, the kids go in and out of your room, they snatch all your things. And you know, you can't really say much to them. You know, telling the kids, like, okay, you're not allowed to come in here when it is their house. And there's no privacy," she said. Living in turns blurry boundaries into no boundaries at all. Depending on your employer, you are always on call. If you are in their house, parents assume you are available. "Since you are living there, it's, like, okay, the parents are going to take a shower, so you have to watch the kids. Okay, the parents are running late so you have to watch the kids. It didn't matter whatever plans I had for myself . . . it was always like I didn't have my own life. I was, like, a slave to them, you know, whatever happened." Serena recalled a dad asking her to watch the kids who were driving him crazy while he finished up a conference call. Then, she says, "I hear the dad snoring in the next room, and I'm, like, thirty minutes later, 'Um, you are not working, you're taking a nap,' but what am I going to do?"

Employers, most often the mother who employs domestic help, may intentionally or unconsciously encourage a blurry boundary between a job and relationship. Hired as hourly workers, domestics are also expected to feel a true attachment to the family, a child, an elderly or disabled family member. And often they do. Through the many stories we gathered from care workers, we often heard about the deep satisfaction they got from enhancing the lives of children or elders in their care. And for the hiring family, such affection ensures better care and loyalty to a vulnerable person's well-being. Care is provided not as a strict checklist but as a response to human needs.

Yet, concurrently, that list must be checked. All designated tasks must be accomplished by the end of the day or by some prescribed period. Dishes must be done, floors swept, clothes washed, and bathrooms cleaned. Or a child must be fed, washed, taken to the park, soothed, and put down for a nap. It emerges as a dual role: in one minute, checking off a list of required duties, and the next, being expected to act as devoted kin. This blurry role can easily expand too. Working in close proximity, particularly over years, domestic and care workers may see a creep in expectations. Deeply embedded in family life in which babies are born, illnesses occur, conflicts arise, or parents' jobs suddenly demand more hours, they may be expected to understand, even have sympathy for, the employing family's changing needs. After a divorce, the nanny may suddenly be in charge of packing up and moving kids between households. House cleaners say they are occasionally—and then routinely—asked to watch a new baby while cleaning. Child minders are asked to do additional "light" housework or to stay late to watch kids. Much of this extra work goes uncompensated because it is *care* work, often done quietly, behind the scenes, inside the home.

Regina, a Black homecare worker, pointed out ways that she and her co-workers offer far more than is ever on paper. "If you are really a good caregiver, you will notice some of the things going on with your client and you will get right in there and try to rearrange something. . . . It's very complicated work; you kind of have to create, you know, sort out a different plan for each person." A patient came to her who was quadriplegic, and, looking through the file, Regina realized her Medicaid benefits were about to run out. "She was getting ready to lose all her help, but here I am, a homecare worker, trying to help. She can't move. I took it upon myself to call down to [the state capital office] to see who I could get to contact this person. But that's not on my list of duties. . . . I didn't get paid," Regina said. Another of her clients was a musician who'd had several strokes and was having trouble regaining use of his hands. "So one night I'm just thinking, Lord, what do I do? I didn't have an answer. Then the next day, I said, I'm going to Goodwill. I found a guitar, bought it, put that guitar in that client's hand to start having him do mobile activities with his hand and getting back his mind, and so we started having therapy. He started playing," she recounted.

Regina also talked about the risk involved providing transportation for disabled people in her care. "You're taking a risk . . . putting your client in your car. But it's a bigger risk if you put your client in a [city] ride van or some type of a shared ride if they're unaware of how to go by themselves." Regina said that "in good conscience" she just can't ignore the dangerous possibility of him getting off the van and wandering the streets. "So, I try to do the transportation," she said. "Okay, you get forty-six cents or something a mile to provide the transportation but more than half of that is gas, you know, because you may have to go to, like, twenty miles away." The effort of helping her client in and out of her aging car, the cost of transportation, and the risk of an accident is all carried by Regina.

Toxic Work Environments

Mothers working in domestic positions told us disturbing stories about the culture they encountered in homes. Homecare workers, women of color particularly, described the disrespect they saw as prevalent in the private spaces of domestic and care work, most often coming from affluent white women. They spoke of the image of maid, server, personal aide, and cleaner that is infused with "low-class" and racist stereotypes. "The kids have hit me. The mom has made comments that have been verbally abusive, you know, just shaming me, and it's, like, I'm here to help you out. I don't know why you have to treat me that way," Serena said, highlighting some of the abuses she's suffered working as a nanny over the years.

Domestic workers caring for wealthy families described the way in which affluence may be steeped in inequality. Parents model behavior, Serena pointed out, and kids pick up on the way parents treat her: the ones who barely say hello and regard her as an employee who clocks in and clocks out versus those who are more friendly and will sit on the couch and talk, asking about her life. Kids often mimic the class behavior of their parents. "Oh my goodness, there have been boys that I walk in and won't even acknowledge that I'm there. It's, like, [I say] 'Hi, hello, how are you doing?' [with no response] or if I tell them it's time to clean up, they are, like, 'No, you clean up, that's your job.'" Serena recalled cooking a big meal, and then she ended up grabbing a bite for herself while she was sitting there, watching them eat. "And the kid says to me, 'Why are you eating? Why are you sitting with us?'"

Not all the employing parents are like this, but some just bark orders. "They don't really want to chat with me, talk to me, nothing." On top of that, parents may have very strict ideas about routines, diets, and ways their kids should spend their time. They want those intensive rules to be upheld even when they are absent. "They're, like, 'This is what the kids have to eat whether they like it or not': give him protein shakes or vitamins and everything." But Serena had little chance of getting kids to eat food they didn't want or to turn the TV off if they hardly considered her to be a person.

Several Black women care workers talked about white employers as stuck "in that old-time" version of how you treat workers inside private homes. In other words, racist ways. Nannies, domestics, and care workers said some families viewed them as female servants—several women used the word "slaves"—who should be ready to meet any need. Personal care workers spoke of arriving at the door and being told to go home and come back the next day, being ordered to clean up stinking cat boxes or dog shit, or being directed by an elderly client's son to serve him lunch, right away. None of these were among their designated duties. We heard about these conditions from women of different races, but Black women care workers would often name what they recognized as the racialized origin of a historically demeaned workforce.

Lisa talked to homecare worker Alina, who described herself as mixed race, in 2020. For fifteen years Alina has been providing at-home care for elderly and disabled people. She keeps only a few clients she knows well. Over the years, Alina has learned to sense racism within "a minute" of entering someone's home and meeting the disabled person and family members. "I've gone to interviews with people that, absolutely, you could just walk in the house and know that you weren't a fit, and that's okay. And then I've heard there are clients that didn't want someone that was Black. I could care less. I don't want somebody who doesn't want me. And then there's been times I've been around somebody, and they accepted me for the job, but you knew how they felt." These clients will accept Alina's care work but beyond that, "It was uncomfortable, and you know what? They're not that much more important than I am," she said.

Alina says that she knows to avoid those families now. If she feels that it's off, she won't take the job. The work can be overwhelming in a close personal space. Alina explained, "I'll do some grocery shopping, then I'll do some cleaning up. Or I need to do some hands-on stuff like medicines and things like that [where I] need to be in their face. I have two special clients that I have to shower, bathe, change wounds, do medicine distribution." Alina kept returning to the level of intimacy these care jobs require. "You have to be close up," she said, "in their face," which was a major challenge during the pandemic. But it is also very hard to do for someone who is a racist.

"One of my [white] clients I had to cut off completely because she was being racist. I knew she was racist before, because I am multi-race. Then, because of the [Black Lives Matter] protests and stuff going on, it just created extra friction. She was one of my favorites. I thought, you know me, I really thought . . . She's eighty-two years old. You know, she's back in the time, of those days. And she got Alzheimer's. So of course her mental capacity is not all well, and I know that going into the job. You know what you're going up against. But she thought I was out there rioting, so she didn't want nothing to do with me," Alina said. Pain in her voice, Alina said it again, softly this time. "*She wanted nothing to do with me.*"

Dee, a homecare worker and chair of the local Service Employees International Union (SEIU) African American Caucus, counseled Alina. "You know, it's not you, Alina. They still have a mental disease of some sort," Dee said. While Alina spoke of the mental disease rooted in dementia, racism was laced through hers and many descriptions of how domestics and care workers were treated.

Sexual Harassment

There are laws against sexual harassment in the workplace. But they seemed irrelevant in the privacy of people's rooms and homes. Serena mentioned dads "making passes at her," and one homecare worker talked about caring for an elderly woman whose son comes by after drinking and "sits there, says shit" while she cares for his mother. "Like about my body," and then "he's, like, brushing against me. I told him there is no reason for you to be putting your hands on me."

Many workers became skilled at quietly resolving these conflictual situations that were potentially risky. Another homecare worker gave an example of an older man with early dementia who would wait for her to come into his room in the assisted living facility where she provided him with care. Then he would grab her or on occasion start masturbating. She'd been trained to "de-escalate" the situation by telling him to stop and get dressed to go down to dinner. When we asked, "Is there someone you can go to, to get support for that behavior?" she answered, "This stuff happens a lot. Especially with younger men who have mental illness issues."

Among dozens of homecare workers who described their jobs to us, roughly half had experienced unwanted touching and sexual harassment, or even assault, while at work. Not one of them said they even had a place to report these incidents. While some women would simply walk out the door right away, others talked about how hard it was to change clients, locations, and schedules, and just to find work. According to Dee, "People have no idea how much we deal with. They don't want to see it. They want us to clean up the shit, literally. Families don't want to deal with that. They want us to stay unseen, to stay quiet. They want us to understand if their grandmother has racist attitudes or their old grandfather likes to grab us when we are at work. We are the ones who are supposed to understand. Well, it's time they understand what we face."

Workplace Without Protections

In a 2019 interview in the *New York Times Magazine*, Ai-jen Poo, the president of the National Domestic Workers Alliance (NDWA), pointed to racism and sexism as infused in the way domestic labor has evolved in the United States: "The first professional domestic workers in this country were enslaved black women," Poo says. "The nation's labor laws were, from the outset, tied to Jim Crow. And with no minimum wage and no ability to bargain—really no legal protections at all—a workforce that was at the time largely made up of African American women was driven even further into the shadows."[3] The very design and image of the domestic workforce reflects institutionalized mistreatment of African American women. And mainstream feminism has done little to protest the system of oppression created as a result of low-income women of color providing cheap labor in affluent homes. In fact, as Kendall Mikka writes in *Hood Feminism*, when feminism is defined by the priorities of affluent white women, the movement itself essentially relies on the "availability of cheap labor in the home from women of color."[4]

Domestic and care job categories, overwhelmingly filled by women and disproportionately by women of color, have been systematically excluded from basic labor protections and fair wage standards. From the 1930s on, alongside farmworkers, domestic laborers—majority Black and Latinx—were cut out of original Fair Labor Standards Act (FLSA) protections and so were denied minimum wage and basic employment standards, such as overtime pay. Domestic workers were excluded from the 1935 National Labor Relations Act, which protects the rights of employees to engage in collective action to advocate for fair treatment and conditions at work. When Congress passed the 1964 Civil Rights Act, again domestic workers were excluded; it wasn't until the 1970s that the FLSA was extended to most categories of domestic labor. However, live-in nannies and eldercare workers are still exempt from basic labor protections. Even the long overdue inclusion of domestic workers in the FLSA has constraints. Workers providing elderly, ill, or disabled people with more than one in five hours of "companionship" lose the right to basic protections including the minimum wage. The way domestic workers have been cut out of policies and protections in the United States reflects global trends. According to the International Labour Organization, a United Nations agency, 36 percent of domestic workers worldwide are still completely excluded from labor law protections. Attention and emotional care of vulnerable people, while presumably so important to families, is the least valued work in the economy.

The National Domestic Workers Alliance was founded in 2007 to advocate for the rights of domestic workers in the United States. Their central mission was the passage of a Domestic Workers Bill of Rights to ensure protection under human rights laws, regulate overtime pay and time off, and provide recourse for workers who suffer sexual and/or racial harassment.[5] Different states have passed their own versions, including New York in 2010. But, among the women we spoke with, we found that enforcement of these protections was completely lacking. We did not come across any women who had reported the labor violations, sexual harassment, or racist treatment and attacks they suffered. Since these women are often living in poverty and may be undocumented or not reporting income, they make a silent calculation, weighing unfair treatment or even abuse—sexual and racist—against the impact to their families of lost income. Several women who worked for wealthy families also recognized the way those families all seemed to know one another, suggesting that a reputation as a problem worker, even if unjustified, could be catastrophic to future job prospects.

The High Ground

"We have our own values."

While many care workers shared stories about the hidden, dark side of domestic labor, we also heard from them about strong, authentic relationships with clients and families. Many of the women, including Alina, Ramona, Celia, and Serena, spoke about the feelings of children, elders, and disabled people in their care, of what it must be like to "be in their shoes." Serena developed close ties with some children that made it difficult to leave them. "You become attached to these kids and they get very attached to you," she said. But for many of the parents, she maintains, "Even if I am not doing anything wrong, they can fire me at any minute. And you know, most of the time the parents won't let me say good-bye to the children, and the children are left wondering, like, where have you been?" Serena remembered seeing one of the kids she used to care for at the YMCA where she was taking her new employer's children. "It's really heartbreaking," she recalls. "They are saying, like, don't you miss me and why don't you come play with me anymore?" Despite the potentially close bonds that can develop between these women and their client, every domestic and care worker recalled experiences of exploitation, mistreatment, and even abuse. Some talked about how to hold on to your own values and survive.

Mariella, a Native American mom from Oregon, said, "It's the values. I don't know if you ever heard the term. You go into the inner body, inner soul. And for your own safety that's the only way you're going to survive. Have you read the stories of Sacagawea? She was pregnant when she came across [thousands of miles of the United States]. Everyone else, they didn't know how she did it. They wanted to know what that secret was, that's what she said. She'd go into her inner body, her inner soul." That's how Mariella describes her strategy to balance the demands of caring for her disabled clients. But she also has a son with bipolar disorder and is deeply concerned for his future. She went on to say, "It's not about race. It's not about money. It's not about your title that you earn through your education or your job, whether you're the president or whether you're a maid. Whatever it is, not about religion. It's about help, helping each other. When the time arises, the need is there." Mariella believes we are all eventually reduced to vulnerability. No matter who you are, that is coming. How we treat those who provide care says a lot about our values, she explained. Other care workers agreed.

Regina discussed the values foundational to her work as a certified homecare worker as she watched almost all of her work disappear during the pandemic. She was convinced that her fragile clients had needs that were not being met. A religious woman, she found herself reflecting on the elders trapped at home. So, she said, "Let me get my heart ready. I saw the need for food, and I started with three families and those were seniors that weren't able to drive and they were eighty to eighty-one and seventy-something. So I just went and started picking up food boxes. . . . I've gone from three to twenty-five families . . . and now they'll call me and say, 'Regina, I don't need no more nothing, thank you so much.'" When asked if she was being paid for this personal version of homecare, she said, "No, I don't get paid for it. I don't get no money. It's just been out of the kindness of my heart. And as a matter of fact, I'll say this, it's been such a blessing to where I haven't even asked." In fact, after a while, all the different low-income families and frontline staff at the buildings where she was delivering food started collecting money to cover her costs and wages. She believed the kindness she sent out came back to her. But that is seldom the case.

Pandemic Care Work

The Center for American Progress documented that, overall, women lost some 5.4 million jobs during the pandemic recession and Black and Latinx women lost the most.[6] Over 2020–21, we heard that Celia, Hilda, Regina, Serena, Ramona, and many others had lost some or all of their incomes during the pandemic. Joyce, a fifty-eight-year-old homecare worker from Oregon who identifies as mixed race, pointed out another cost to their families. "I have one client, in a facility, who has dementia, advanced dementia, and she, you know, she's in a wheelchair, but she, I mean she's clueless. You could tell her a million times [to keep a mask on] and, like, she, she doesn't know what's going on to tell her. But you know every-one expects you to go on and take care of her. Her family and the staff. I've known her for years, and I want to make sure she's getting the care. But it's, like, 'What about the risk to me?' But, I thought if I say, 'No I can't risk this'. . . and I have asthma, well you know I could just lose that job too. I lost half my income over COVID."

She and other homecare workers pointed out that they could also be bringing the pandemic home. "I have a partner who's immunocompromised. I take care of my ninety-year-old mother on the weekends. We are being asked to go into homes where there's no mask wearing and what have you, we bring that home." The SEIU pushed hard for the state to provide homecare workers with masks, sanitizer, and other personal protective equipment (PPE), in order to maintain the safest conditions possible during the pandemic. However, the true complexity of caring for little children and mentally disabled people who don't have the capacity to understand the risk they pose by not wearing a mask was off-loaded onto careworkers, primarily women, with their own vulnerable family members to worry about. Joyce and others pointed out that the history of exploiting homecare workers is so much a part of affluent culture that "it took COVID to get some people to see it." Still, while PPE was brought in from all over the world and distributed to doctors and nurses, care workers waited many months to be recognized as frontline or health care workers, a move that put the most important people in these women's lives—their children—at risk.

4

The Centrality of Motherhood

"For your kids, you just figure out how to make things work."

Joanna was a nurse in Ireland before she moved to the United States with her husband and young son, while pregnant with her daughter. Now in her sixties, she speaks quickly with a clipped Irish accent and a self-deprecating cackle. Not long after arriving in the states, her family had settled into a house in Quincy, Massachusetts, a Boston suburb. Over the years, they added another child to the brood, but the marriage faltered and her husband took off. "He was having an affair with one of my best friends," she recalled. "We got no child support from him, nothing from him really, just a lot of shame about my situation. I didn't really know how things worked in this country. I did get the house, but I had to figure out how to make it work as a single mum." Now Joanna can remember, with more laughter than pain, building a life in a new country with her kids at the center; the only way to do this was to find a job that fit around their needs. "For your kids, you just figure out how to make things work," she said.

Kids were at the center of almost every mother's account we

heard over the years. Given wage poverty and layers of precarious circumstances, these mothers' lives orbited around meeting kids' needs. Joanna's history echoes this priority. Back in
Ireland, Joanna had a college degree in child psychology and
nursing credentials. But to work as a registered nurse in the
United States, she would have had to return to school. With
young kids at home, no help, and little money, going back to
school wasn't an option. So instead of getting paid as a nurse,
Joanna found work as a patient advocate or home health aide
through local agencies doing in-home care for elderly clients.
Even today, home health aides and nursing assistants in the
United States make on average between $10 and $19 per hour,
whereas nurses make an average of $34 an hour. But doing
at-home care allowed her to choose shifts around the kids'
schedules: "I chose this line of work because it was so flexible
that it didn't affect the kids at all—their sports, their school,
their homework. I started taking overnight shifts because then
I would be home to get them ready and off to school in the
mornings, and I'd be there for after school too." Finding someone to spend the night could be tricky, so Joanna flew her sister
in from Ireland to help watch the kids overnight. "I was very
lucky. It was supposed to be for six months, but she ended
up moving in with me for five years," They kept struggling
to make ends meet, though, partially because these agencies
offered no benefits.

Many of the moms talked about searching for work they
could mold around their kids' schedules, which often resulted
in creative living arrangements. When her kids were four, ten,
and eleven, Joanna's household became even more blended by

design. "I was taking care of these two elderly sisters in a nursing home. It wasn't a good situation, and so I decided to move them into my house with us. . . . I figured out how to do it. I won guardianship of the sisters, and they had a house, so they were able to sell the house to pay for the in-home care. It just worked." Joanna remembers all of them eating dinner together. This setup allowed Joanna to be home for her kids in a field where "work from home" was unheard of. "It didn't interfere with their lives, sports, and school and all of that, and of course it meant I was able to be around more. . . . They [elderly sister clients] spent many years at my house, and it worked out really well until the very end."

Joanna's kids are now in their thirties, and she is a proud grandmother of four. Her son is an electrician and her oldest daughter is a single mom of two, working her way through nursing school. Her youngest daughter, Katie, struggled for years as an addict and received disability benefits due to the physical damage from years of hard living. When Katie's son Trevor was a toddler and Katie was in the throes of addiction, Joanna had taken over partial guardianship with Trevor's father. Amanda met Joanna and her cherubic grandson in 2011. During lunch at the local Ninety Nine restaurant, Joanna set up her grandson with toys and snacks in the booth. Joanna talked about scheduling homecare shifts around childcare needs during the time Trevor spent at her house. Today, Trevor is fourteen and lives out of state with his dad. "We're still very close. We have that unbreakable kind of bond from when he was with me," Joanna said on the phone, her voice catching.

Asked about the toll of a lifetime of caring for people, Joanna said, "I loved doing it. It was my world." Even in her sixties, after a second bout with cancer and only a few months out from a delicate surgery to excise a tumor from her mouth, which required the removal of all her teeth, Joanna is back to working three days a week. She takes full pandemic precautions due to the impact of chemotherapy on her immune system, but her finances wouldn't allow for more than a few weeks off. "I work because I have to, you know, to pay the bills, but I still love it . . . caring for people," she said. Through her cancer treatment, roles were reversed, and she needed help from her kids. "The doctor says I'm very determined, like a fighter, but I'm also a private person. And my kids have been the ones who could really be there for me, and that means everything."

The women we spoke with prided themselves on prioritizing their kids. In their now famous study of low-income mothers in Philadelphia, researchers Kathryn Edin and Maria Kefalas found that because of their limited educational and work opportunities, low-income women placed extreme value on motherhood and viewed their kids as the main source of contribution and achievement in their lives.[1] Similarly, many of the moms here strove to fulfill the intensive mothering ideal that has come to dominate culturally. They wanted to be present to get kids off the school bus, supervise homework, and fill schedules with enriching activities. Moms also knew that teachers, coaches, and school administrators expected them to be present for school meetings and events. However, since these moms did not have the resources available to support this model of intensive parenting, they had to get creative.

At-Home Daycare: Combining Work and Care

Watching other people's kids in your home allows the ultimate flexibility to care for your own kids while still getting paid. June, a white mom of three boys from Michigan, had never planned to open a daycare; for years, she'd been a stay-at-home mom and dabbled in real estate as a leasing agent. But suddenly, she needed to escape an abusive situation with her then-husband and father of her kids. "My boys were the reason I left. I'm not going to let them be raised in an environment like that," June explained. They fled with nothing, relying on support from June's family and advice from a lawyer and advocate at the women's shelter. "We ran to my parents' house. Literally threw stuff into a trash bag, grabbed the dog . . . my kids, car seats, just grabbed stuff and ran out of the house." They even dropped off the car in a nearby lot, knowing she couldn't afford the insurance and not wanting him to come after them to get their only car back. "That was it. I mean we had no money from him. My sister would even take me on grocery sprees. And I was so thankful I would cry . . . he even took away my bank account, so I was just selling stuff, whatever I could," she said.

June's kids needed her more than ever before, especially since her older son "knows more and has seen more" and was struggling. At the same time, she had to find a job to support them. Despite having a bachelor's degree and conducting an exhaustive job hunt, June could not find any work that would financially and practically allow for care of her kids. "I went around, applying for all of these jobs, they were, like, 'Oh, you are too experienced or you would cost us too much money.' And they didn't have any thoughts about my three kids, like, whatever kind of care I would find for them while I worked. They didn't care," she said. Even applying for childcare jobs, June was shocked they didn't offer placements or compensation for her own kids while she would be working. No job would pay as much as childcare would cost for her three young kids.

Like many of the moms we talked to, by the time June found herself in this moment of crisis, she had already racked up decades of childcare experience. "I'd been working in child-care for, you know, pretty much all my life," she said. So she decided to do the only thing that would allow her to earn a living while caring for her kids. "I started my own business, a daycare in my home." Her mom, who lived in Pittsburgh, moved in with June and the boys in Michigan while she did the background testing, certification, and license acquisition necessary to get her daycare up and running. "My family was totally instrumental in helping me," said June. "Moms are ingenious really, if you ask me; they just find a way to survive," she said, acknowledging her mother's sacrifice and her own fierce determination to be there for her sons.

For the first few years running the daycare, her two young-est kids were under seven so they counted against the limit of six children per caregiver in a home daycare setting. But combined with food assistance and Medicaid, payment from four children was enough for them to live on. Most impor-tant, June molded the daycare's daily schedule around her own kids' needs. "When we started, my oldest was in the first grade, so we just incorporated it and, like, we all walked together to the bus stop. My middle was in preschool, so that is a half day, so we'd walk to the bus stop in the morning, at the half day, and then at the end of the day, and those were our daily walks with the kids in the daycare. It gave me peace of mind, because I'm not just sending my kids out there alone." She was even equipped to handle when her kids got sick. "The house is totally wide open, so I can hear and see almost anything, and if I need to put them up in their room, then I'll make sure everybody is safe and chill and then go running with more ginger ale, crackers, whatever they need. Or maybe we'll do a resting day with the rest of the kids where we watch a movie, or if I have a sick kid who really wants to be on the couch, which has happened before, I'll take the other kids out back, because we have a fully fenced yard. And there is a bolt lock and a house alarm, so we are all safe." It was clear talking to June that the horror of finding her husband with gas cans and a gun safe, which she worried were meant to harm the family, still haunts her years later. Working from home allows June to keep a near-constant eye on her kids, the only thing that calms her worry.

Finding Flexible Arrangements at Work and Home

Creativity for working moms takes many forms. Tilly, an Oregon single mom of two, teamed up with another single mom to raise their kids together after they'd both experienced breakups. Tilly told Lisa that it was an unconventional living arrangement but it worked for more than ten years through rentals, evictions, and eventually purchasing a home. "When one of us worked graveyard, or even when, you know, she wanted to go out with some girlfriends, go out for a drink, she could just leave the door open after the kids went to sleep. And then I would just keep an ear out," Tilly said. "That's the sense of freedom that I got. I mean, she, we, really kind of just raised each other's kids, you know; we raised each other's kids together, which is also nice to feel like somebody else loves your children." She admits the arrangements kept them from pursuing serious romantic relationships while they were living together. But it was the best for the kids, and that's what mattered most to both moms.

Other moms we met managed to mold working lives around care for their kids. Jesse, a white single mom of a five-year-old daughter in Connecticut, was excited to uncover a new career path as a firefighter. "Not too long ago, I ended up realizing the career change I really wanted to do was firefighting. So I actually did an EMT course for firefighting, and I became a volunteer firefighter on a search and rescue team in Hartford. I've taken the written exam and applied to every possible job. The last two years, that's been the thing I am focused on—it's the golden one," said Jesse, with palpable enthusiasm.

> **Amanda:** When you were growing up, did you want to be a firefighter?

> **Jesse:** No, honestly it all happened because I met a firefighter in the park who was playing with his daughter. And he just talked about how it was such a great job, and I never realized firefighters only work two days a week in Connecticut. So, as a single mom, the idea of only working two days a week, even if it's a twenty-four-hour shift, it's just such a benefit, and then, you know, you get all the other benefits like unlimited sick leave and the pension.

Jesse had come to believe that firefighting would be the perfect job for a single parent like her who had family support to cover overnights.

> Amanda: It seems what you are aspiring to in terms of your career is a job that will allow you to be a mom?

> Jesse: Oh definitely. I've been working since I was eleven, not a real job, just at a concession stand down the street. And then when I was fifteen, I got my first real job. And all my life since then, I've just been working multiple jobs . . . until I had my daughter, and then everything changed. Now she comes first. I'd rather spend time with her, and just make ends meet, you know?

By the spring of 2020, Jesse had passed the firefighters exam and was waiting for positions to open up at fire departments in the area where she lived with her daughter. "Now that COVID hit, I can't be there [volunteer firefighting]. I used to be every day, and it's not that I don't want to be." Even if the opportunity to go to the fire academy arose during the pandemic, Jesse said she didn't have the childcare from family she would need to be able to go. So at least for the moment, Jesse's dreams of becoming a firefighter stood suspended.

Across the country, when school provided reliable childcare, we often heard from women searching for jobs with "mother's hours" because this enabled a kid-centered lifestyle. In 2012, Amanda met Jamie, a Latinx Boston mom of three, with a baby on the way. They chatted in a spare room full of long tables and stacks of chairs in the Boston public school where Jamie worked; she talked about cobbling together part-time positions with local nonprofits and the Boston Public Schools doing community outreach. Jamie said she liked working with kids "a lot better than adults." And this job gave her that coveted "8 to 3" school day schedule; at times, she even worked in the same building as her children. Though Jamie was regarded as a hard worker and prized employee because of her ability to connect with Spanish-speaking parents, she went without benefits and job security since her positions were paid through grants. "I know that right now we have funding through September, and my baby is due in the summer," she said. Although Jamie qualified for sick leave through her position, which she planned to use after she gave birth, she did not have any maternity or parental leave. "If you are a teacher in the public schools, there are a lot of things you can qualify for, but for us, we don't have a union," Jamie said. Many of the moms we talked with considered jobs with benefits, union eligibility, and room for promotion as something they hoped to pursue when their kids were older.

Likewise, in 2011, we met Roberta, a white single mom of an eight-year-old son who was living in public housing in South Boston and participating in a social mobility program designed to empower low-income single moms. In the booth of an empty pub over salads for lunch, Roberta pulled out her phone to show Amanda photos of her son in his basketball uniform. She admitted the empowerment program counselors were disappointed she was searching for a job with hours that would allow her to get her son off the bus, drive him to sports practices, and help with homework. While getting to do these things may have made Roberta a better mom, the program focused on helping the women achieve "self-sufficiency" by furthering their education and finding highly paid jobs. Getting her son off the bus was not helping in this way. Partly because of her limited availability, Roberta was searching for openings in school settings and piecing together part-time jobs in the meantime.

Often moms chose to sacrifice higher wages and the possibility of promotion in exchange for the temporary flexibility they needed to be good parents. Kara, a white mom of three, had been working in an entry-level position in the corporate world, but after a divorce, her kids needed more of her attention. Amanda talked to Kara over coffee in the kitchen of the public housing unit she shared with her kids in a tree-lined Boston suburb. Kara talked about the choice to move from her job in corporate human resources to work for her uncle because of the flexibility working for family allowed. But there were trade-offs. "It was not corporate so there were no benefits . . . no sick days, no personal time, no benefits. I only got paid $13 an hour. But it had the benefit of the fact that it was family, so that if I needed, I could bring my kid into work with me for a little bit. Or [leave] if I needed to pick up." Kara made the sacrifice we heard countless moms describe: economic hardship in the short term in order to focus on kids while they are young.

While jobs with school-day or flexible hours were relatively hard to find unless the women were working for family members or as part of the school system, overnight shifts always seemed to be available. For moms who lived with extended family or had parents or grandparents who could sleep over, these jobs offered the freedom to be present when kids were awake, even if that meant being around but exhausted. Like several of the moms in the previous chapters, when asked when she slept, Sandra, a Latinx single mom of three young kids, answered "not much." To accommodate the ever-changing needs of her school-aged daughters and her eighteen-month-old son, she worked two to three overnight shifts per week in a local warehouse. This allowed her to be home during the day to handle school and daycare issues and doctor appointments.

Nighttime care by family members made it possible for many of the moms to take overnight shifts, but COVID was devastating to these arrangements. Jesse was forced to quit an overnight warehouse job she'd recently started when the pandemic hit, because her grandmother who had been staying over had underlying health conditions that put her at risk. In a study of working single moms during the pandemic, researchers found that low-income mothers who had previously relied on family members for childcare, but did not live in the same household as the caregivers, suffered the worst disruption to their work and care arrangements.[2]

In 2020, Luisa, a Latinx single mom, was managing a European Wax Center on Long Island, New York. But the pay wasn't enough to support her first-grade twins without help, so she relied on daycare vouchers and public health insurance for the boys. Like most of the single moms we met, she received no child support from her sons' father. Very few poor mothers file for and receive child support; in our research, more common was under-the-table ad hoc assistance from fathers in the form of gifts and occasional babysitting, which Luisa also described.[3] Eventually, she hoped to go back to school to pursue a degree in nursing.

As the pandemic shut down spa locations nationwide, Luisa

got a call to interview for a job at CityMD, an urgent care clinic, as an after-care clinical assistant. In this position, she would follow up with patients after appointments to answer questions, help with referrals, and pass along lab reports. The pay wasn't great, but Luisa saw the potential to gain experience in the medical field and to work from home since most of their operations were now remote. "It was so helpful to be able to be home with the kids . . . challenging also," she said, laughing. Helpful because the boys were attending school virtually but challenging because they were sitting next to her, asking for things. Luisa chose to keep the boys online even after their school went back to full-time in-person learning for the remainder of the school year in 2021, because it was easier to manage. "Virtual is helpful, because, you know, I don't have to rush and go pick them up if I have something going on at work like happened today," she said. The ability to work from home may be especially helpful for single parents, but most mothers in low-income America aren't given a remote option. In fact, research shows that the ability to work from home varied sharply by socioeconomic class even before COVID, and the pandemic exacerbated the divide.

Pandemic Hurdles

In 2020, with daycares and schools essentially shut down, many moms were left "working" twenty-four hours a day; growing recognition emerged of the intense labor undertaken by women caring for kids and home. Pre-pandemic, Danielle and her fiancé scheduled their job hours around care of their four kids. By switching off work schedules, they "never had to use outside childcare," which is a feat itself. "No matter where [I] and my fiancé work, we always did a separate schedule, so, like, for a while he did the third shift and I did the first. So it's me or him always there with the kids, or back when we were living with my mom, it could be her, so you know we never had an issue with childcare." But homeschooling during the pandemic shutdown created new challenges; with their three-year-old at home and the older kids homeschooling during the day, someone had to be present to coordinate. "I start work at 4 a.m. and I get off at 12:30 p.m. So he does the mornings, and then I come home and give him a break, but if he were working too, our schedules would collide, and then there would be nobody here in the morning for a couple of hours, so obviously we can't do that. So we had to sacrifice and give up his job for now." This means less money coming in, but the kids are always cared for, which according to Danielle is "the most important thing."

When Amanda spoke to Danielle in the winter of 2020, she talked about changing her work schedule to coordinate with her three-year-old's classroom Zoom. She wanted to participate in some of the Head Start classes with her daughter, but this reduced Danielle's available work hours, and hers was the only paycheck coming in. "It affects me negatively because now I'm losing four hours a week. To the average person, it might seem like that's not a lot. But to me, that's a lot. That's like $70 I'm losing a week; to the average person who is living paycheck to paycheck, it's a lot."

Five years after opening, June's daycare is still up and running. But the pandemic created a big challenge to the viability of her business and her family's ability to scrape by. "I didn't have any kids coming here for three full months from March until June, whenever that ban was lifted. The only way we were able to survive was because I had two families who were full timers who decided to keep paying me full price. They didn't have to do that, but they were just so understanding, and that's how we survived those three months," she said. Eventually, they also received her ex-husband's stimulus check and part of his unemployment payments, which were garnished, but the payments didn't arrive during those difficult pandemic months.

COVID also forced June to become more flexible with her daycare program model. Instead of accepting a majority of children whose parents work full time during regular business hours, June now takes more kids for shorter time periods throughout the day and week. "Parents are working again, but many of them are home or not working full time, so they'll keep the kids home more to save money. So they are all coming at different times. There are like four of them doing virtual school here at the house. Then two of them do virtual school at home and come here in the afternoons, and they are all different ages. But I got to the point where I was just so desperate for kids, I was just saying yes to everybody, to all these different arrangements. Now every day of the week is different."

Across the nation, the pandemic created a crisis for childcare providers and parents; the degree of permanent damage to the childcare industry remains to be seen. When asked in 2020, two out of five childcare providers said they would close permanently without further government assistance.[4] Among the centers that stayed open, more than 80 percent said they were enrolling fewer kids and four in ten reported taking on personal debt, like loans and credit cards, in order to survive.[5] Even before the pandemic, two-thirds of daycare centers in the United States were small businesses serving fewer than seventy-five kids and struggling to make ends meet, according to the U.S. Chamber of Commerce Foundation.

A few years ago, June had been able to fill her spots just through word of mouth. "I used to have a waiting list, and then all of the sudden it was bone dry. I've never gone so long without kids. I was getting worried and advertising all over the place." She believes when things get back to normal with the virus, she'll be able to have a more regular schedule with full-time kids. With her youngest ready to go off to school in the fall of 2021, June says her daycare could pull in more income than ever before because "I'll be able to fill every spot for the first time." June hopes her reputation in the community will keep her from being among the half of daycare centers that researchers suggest may close permanently due to the pandemic, resulting in an estimated 4.5 million lost childcare slots across the nation.[6] We talk in-depth about the childcare dilemma for parents and workers in chapter 5.

Stay-at-Home Mothering as a Choice

COVID forced mothers across the country to "stay-at-home" because suddenly their kids were stuck there, unattended. But over the last several decades, mothers at opposite ends of the income spectrum have been the most likely to stop out of the workforce in order to care for young children. It is perhaps the most obvious way to treat motherhood as a priority, but culturally, stay-at-home parenting may be viewed as an option available only to affluent families. For many of the poor moms we talked to, weighing the needs of their kids against bad job options, the math just doesn't work. The cost of living calculation, including childcare for young children, would wipe out any paycheck they could bring home. So despite all of the powerful cultural messages telling poor mothers they must go to work, some choose to stay home while their kids are young. Robert Monahan, executive director of Julie's Family Learning Center in South Boston, which offers poor mothers skills training while kids attend Montessori preschool, says staying home as full-time parents makes sense for some mothers. "Some of the people who come through our program, we help them to apply to community college or get into the trades, but there are mothers who are going to continue receiving benefits and remain full-time parents." In fact, roughly one quarter of stay-at-home parents are living in poverty.[7] Their wages tend to be so low and the cost of childcare so high that, if they can piece together some way to scrape by, staying home makes sense.

Often staying home to care for kids does not mean leaving the workforce altogether; among the moms we met, the "stop out" tended to be partial or temporary. Jesse made the choice to withdraw from the workforce and stay at home when her daughter was two, and then she returned when her daughter turned four and became eligible for pre-K programs. "I decided to stay at home with my daughter . . . it was hard as a single parent when I was working full time. I would get maybe an hour and a half in the morning with her, and then I'd have to leave for work, which was about an hour drive in traffic. I'd work like eight to ten hours, and my parents would pick up from daycare, and I'd get like an hour when I got home before she went to bed," Jesse explained. It would have been different, she said, if the crazy back-and-forth meant they could live comfortably, but she was still falling short on her monthly bills. "Even then, like, I work all day and daycare costs $1,400 a month, so between that and bills, it's not even enough, and my parents would have to help me." While staying home with her daughter, she was able to collect unemployment, and although they had less money, she said the time together was worth it. "We'd go to the zoo and swimming and on hikes, plus hip-hop on Mondays, ballet on Tuesdays, gymnastics on Wednesdays."

But poor moms may worry how their choice will be perceived. "I hated when people asked me, 'What do you do for work?' It's like that voice in my head saying I don't do anything, but that's not true. I just don't have a husband to pay for everything, but every cent I have goes to my daughter," Jesse admitted. In Fairfield County, where Jesse and her daughter live, rates of mothers who are stay-at-home parents are some of the highest nationwide because of the concentration of wealth in the suburbs surrounding New York City. While the Pew Center reported that around 20 percent of American families have one stay-at-home parent, the rates in some towns in Fairfield County and neighboring Westchester County, New York, approach double the national average.[8] The vast majority of these stay-at-home parents are women whose husbands make more than enough to pay the bills. Jesse knew that, while the wealthy version of stay-at-home was revered or at least supported, she would be tagged as irresponsible for staying home with her children.

Jesse's observation that women who stay home with their children are seen by many as "doing nothing" reflects the cultural denigration of gendered care work. Trivializing this labor that holds families and communities intact and functioning impacts society at all levels. But there is a profound difference between the lives of wealthy and poor mothers when staying home. In fact, wealthy stay-at-home parents often rely on the domestic labor of poor women whose stories we heard in chapter 3. More than 95 percent of house cleaners and 97 percent of childcare workers are female, and many domestic workers are forced to leave their own kids at home to go to work.[9] Not all wealthy women are oblivious to this paradox. Several of the affluent moms we talked to felt guilty about employing moms who would presumably rather be spending time with their own kids. Laura, a white former attorney in Manhattan now living in Darien, Connecticut, with her husband and three kids, relied on household help as she transitioned from part time to staying home. "My husband was begging me to stay home, because our life was just completely out of control. . . . And I was, like, I want to keep my babysitter, you know, because frankly, my husband wasn't really in a position to really help me," she said. In the United States, high-level executive positions tend to be all-consuming and held primarily by men; seven out of ten of the top wage-earning men have a stay-at-home spouse.[10]

Laura's family employed a live-in nanny for seven years when the kids were growing up, even while Laura stayed at home. They grew close, "like family," Laura said. But she and her husband were uncomfortable with the knowledge that the nanny was working to send money to her kids who lived across the globe and just wanted her to come home. "My husband and I discussed it, and we were, like, 'Listen, her family is depending on her, and if she doesn't work for us she's going to work for somebody else, and we have a really nice relationship, you know?'" Laura explained, clearly conflicted. "I remember there were conversations where she [their nanny] would be upset. She'd be, like, 'You know my daughter says you always say one more year or it's always going to be this year, and then it's never the right time.'" Their nanny did finally return home after more than a decade working in the United States. "You know, her children went to the fanciest school, private school. And now she has an apartment . . . and this gorgeous country house. And she never has to work again." What hangs in the silence, talking on the phone to Laura, is all the time the nanny and her children missed and can never get back.

Part of the reason Laura decided to stay home was because her daughter had been diagnosed with developmental delays and required various therapies and appointments. "My oldest had some language delays and some developed developmental disabilities, and with a special needs child, navigating the whole, you know, eligibility process for special ed services. I wouldn't say it's a full-time job, but that really took up a lot of time between all of the appointments and the therapies and trying to get the services from the school district," Laura said.

A surprising number of the low-income mothers we talked to said one of their children had special needs, and all of those moms recognized the overwhelming burden this placed on the family. In two of the three studies for which we tracked this data, more than half of the women said they had at least one child with special needs. Although there are problematic elements of the process in which poor kids are disproportionately identified as needing special education or disciplinary measures in schools, what we heard from the mothers was how difficult it was to get help for their kids.[11] Many of the moms described dealing with kids' serious medical, health, and behavioral issues with little assistance while, at the same time, struggling to bring home a paycheck. After her four-year-old was diagnosed with uncontrolled type 1 diabetes, Sandra, a low-income single mom living in Delaware, said she felt swamped by all of the appointments and monitoring her daughter suddenly required. Because her daughter sometimes became urgently ill at school, Sandra had a difficult time finding daycare and school programs that would accept her. Now her daughter attends a school attached to a local hospital that provides on-site monitoring, but Sandra described always watching her phone and being unable to return to work full time. "This disease has cost me work and homes," she said.

Households with kids can be difficult for anyone to manage, especially when you add in childhood illness or developmental delays. Sabrina, a white, affluent, stay-at-home mom of a son with neurobehavioral challenges, pointed out that getting help is difficult no matter who you are. "It is so time consuming, dealing with the behaviors at home and then the school and the doctors—just to get the diagnosis and doing the therapies, then adjusting the meds. And we have the resources and the insurance to be able to pay for it. I have no idea how people do it when they don't." Sabrina's reflection on how much harder it must be for poor mothers was common among the affluent women we interviewed. Over the years, her son has been diagnosed with a range of special needs from anxiety to bipolar disorder. "He's the reason I haven't been able to go back to work, paid work anyway, full time because it's basically

something that I am dealing with on and off, like, all the time."
A few weeks before Amanda talked to Sabrina in the summer
of 2021, the nurse from her son's sleepaway camp had called.
Her son was having a breakdown and needed to be picked up.
Sabrina's own summer plans were suddenly canceled. Yet the
ability to drop everything to tend to your child is reserved for
those with money.

When the Kids Grow Up . . .

In the spring of 2021, starting to recover from the pandemic
losses to her daycare, June still relies on Medicaid and food
stamps. She is also enrolled in a Michigan program that gives
scholarships to daycare providers to pursue degrees; it's part
of an effort to improve the quality of early childhood education in the state. And June works to increase the star rating
of her daycare center, which goes up when providers show
they are doing things like earning degrees and certifications,
maintaining records of parent communications, and posting
information online or on bulletin boards. "This program gives
me benefits; you have to work harder for them and to keep
them, but that's okay because it's worth it, and it's keeping us
afloat. I'm definitely going to finish my master's degree, so that
is pretty cool." In this way, June's story stood out. For most
moms, the jobs they took that allowed them to focus on their
young kids did not offer opportunities to move up and go back
to school.

Once her daycare years are over, June said, she would like
to "help people" to escape from abusive situations. "Like helping them realize their strength as mothers. I'd like to counsel

victims of domestic violence and help them get out. Find a way to work with their families, maybe as a public speaker." She knows how hard it is to escape abuse. She listened to endless YouTube videos and podcasts about domestic violence when she was trying to find the strength to leave. "I'd love to do public speaking and help to pull people out of those situations, because I know I did it on my own and then you need help to heal." Many of the moms we met hoped to pursue careers "helping people," often in ways they needed help over the years. We heard this message repeatedly: that rather than get lost in despair, they wanted to become people who could change other lives.

When asked about her plans for the future, Sandra at first seemed taken aback as though it was hard to imagine having plans. "Well, I would like to get into a GED program. I would love to go to college and work in the foster care system . . . someday. I could work with them as a counselor or something overnight or as an administrative assistant or something," she said. Sandra had been in and out of foster care growing up. "But I just couldn't imagine working, going to school, and being a full-time mom in my situation," she continued, drawn back in by her current situation. "It just seems so hard right now. I don't know if it would be possible."

Feminists have long worried about the impact of the five- or ten-year "nap" that motherhood may require, delaying moms' career development to care for kids. And feminist economists have highlighted the ways in which responsibility for care work at home disadvantages women economically. But mainstream feminist analyses tend to focus on white women who are middle- and upper-income educated professionals. In *Hood*

Feminism, Mikka Kendall writes, "We rarely talk about basic needs as a feminist issue. Food insecurity and access to quality education, safe neighborhoods, a living wage, and medical care are all feminist issues. Instead of a framework that focuses on helping women get basic needs met, all too often the focus is not on survival but on increasing privilege."[12]

For poor mothers who are disproportionately women of color, putting off career ambitions often starts when they are just girls, and continues until their children have grown up. These moms may be in their forties or fifties before they are able to start focusing on themselves. And as we've seen, by this time they are often drawn back in by other family responsibilities, including the care of grandkids. Some, however, do find a way to move up and out from under the overwhelming burden of poverty and care work. When they do, the path they often choose is a career committed to working with other low-income families, still trapped in wage poverty.

5

The Broken Promise of Childcare

"Kids have to be somewhere."

A key part of the plan to end welfare was, according to then presidential candidate Bill Clinton, the promise to "empower people with the education, training and child care they need" to move up and out of poverty.[1] Politicians promised high-quality, subsidized childcare to enable poor mothers to discover the "dignity of work," because suddenly the work they were doing in their homes, caring for kids, no longer counted. But the availability of childcare has never come close to meeting the need. Today, most states serve only between 5 and 25 percent of eligible families who qualify for childcare subsidies. Sheila Katz, a white professor at the University of Houston and an expert on women's poverty and social welfare, explained: "With welfare reform, the politicians became much more interested in forcing women to work, and then kind of offering child care while they worked, but that child care was never comprehensive enough to care for their kids."

Across the country, we heard moms complain about incredibly long wait lists, especially for spots in subsidized daycare centers. One low-income mom in Denver explained she's only able to work five hours a day until her daughter gets off a waiting list for after-school care. "She's on four wait lists. But I can't leave a seven-year-old alone. I broke down this week." One reason centers cite for not accepting subsidies are the set rates for care allowed by the subsidy program in each state. If the market supports much higher tuition costs (and the center has a waiting list of potential full-payers), there is little incentive to absorb the financial loss of taking a child with a voucher, which may be several hundred dollars a month.

Childcare aid for low-income families consists of means-tested or income-eligibility vouchers, Head Start, and pre-K programs. Childcare is not an entitlement program like Social Security or veterans benefits. When childcare money runs out, they start waiting lists. Only about 40 percent of eligible children get into Head Start and early Head Start programs, and with thousands of families on wait lists, many will never get off.[2] Other federal aid for childcare provided through tax credits never reaches low-income families because care has to be paid for up front.[3] The insufficient public childcare system (or lack thereof) in the United States stands in contrast to European countries that invest heavily in universal programs that serve all children.[4] Even affluent families struggle to find daycare openings, especially in major metropolitan areas where parents sign up children months before they are born.

The United States may find a model for high-quality universal public childcare for three- and four-year-olds in Portland, Oregon, starting in the fall of 2022.[5] In 2020, Multnomah County passed a ballot measure approving a tax on the wealthy to fund a year-round childcare and preschool program for all resident children in this age bracket. Portland's plan includes options ranging from home to center-based care in different languages and locations around the county. All kids may attend up to six hours per day free of charge; kids from low-income families receive up to ten hours per day and priority enrollment. Different locations offer evening and weekend hours. The measure passed with wide-ranging public support, perhaps in part because of the aim to serve all children. Mary King, a white professor of economics at Portland State University and public childcare expert and advocate, described the public support she observed before the vote. "Parents really seemed to have an understanding that child care is not affordable for most people. So that, you know, it's a real issue for middle-class families, as well as lower-income families, to pay for child care, despite the fact that you can't make a decent living doing it."

Women like June who serve as daycare providers, preschool teachers, and babysitters are some of the lowest-paid workers in America, though they provide what moms universally recognize as the most important service. Around 95 percent of childcare workers are women and they are disproportionately women of color, according to the Economic Policy Institute. The median wage for childcare workers is around $10 an hour, compared to $17 for workers in other occupations. One in seven are living in poverty, and they are much less likely than other workers to have benefits at work, with 85 percent of childcare workers reporting they do not receive health insurance coverage from their jobs.[6] Universal childcare in Portland stands out partially because of the plan to increase the salaries of all childcare workers, including classroom aides and teaching assistants, to a minimum of around $20 an hour. These are not just public school employees who are a part of a union but includes in-home daycare providers and aides. Programs like the one in Portland are rare, but they show the possibility of treating children as a community priority—ultimately perhaps as a national priority.

Even with incremental progress, gaps will persist. There is wide-ranging public support for proposals on the local and nationals levels to expand public schooling to include a pre-school component for three- and four-year-olds. But there is much less public conversation and support for expanding opportunities and assistance for infant care, which is even more expensive and harder to find than care for older kids. According to Professor King, "The people in the campaign I was working with very much see preschool as the first and easi-est step. The next thing that is absolutely necessary is zero to two [years old] . . . both because it's a huge crying need and so expensive, so challenging, and because there's the recognition that once you have a better paid universal preschool program, even fewer providers are going to offer infant and toddler care."

The State of Public Care

In contrast to valuing childcare, mothers offered detailed accounts of problems accessing and relying on the current system of childcare "assistance." They reported filling out mountains of paperwork to apply, certify, and recertify qual-ifications for a voucher. Since the amount of the voucher is adjusted by income, moms would continuously report their earnings, which caused trouble when hours fluctuated as they often did. Fran, a single mother of two young children living in public housing in Boston, said, "It's hard to get hired when you are a parent, but I need to get a job first to get a voucher for her to go to daycare" in order to go to work. Caught in a similar dilemma, Jesse tried to enroll her daughter in the childcare assistance program in Connecticut called Care 4 Kids but discovered she made too much. "I think it was like $16 extra a month or something over the limit, so they wouldn't give it to me." But after leaving that job, she also couldn't qualify for a Care 4 Kids voucher until she had lined up another job, which was impossible without childcare arrangements.

Even after securing a childcare voucher, finding a provider who would accept the voucher was equally challenging. In fact, we met several low-income moms providing childcare services out of their homes in chapter 3 who had difficulty enrolling kids with subsidies because of the paperwork nightmare and problems the ever-changing subsidies created for providers. Aurora, a single mom of an eight-year-old son, moved from Montana to California when she was accepted into an apprenticeship program to learn a trade. She told Lisa that it seemed like the perfect opportunity to get her little family on its feet. "I was accepted into that program, and I did have a support system in place, but it fell through," she said. "I needed childcare which started between 4:30 and 5 a.m.; I had to drop him off. . . . And I gotta be there on Monday. I literally looked online, and was just looking for someone that would accept government assistance childcare, which is what I had." Aurora could not find any providers with openings that would take her voucher. "Why do all these places refuse to take the state money? Because they are not really about helping a single mom make it," she said. Later in the conversation, though,

Aurora speculated it was probably because the state requires too much paperwork and makes it hard for childcare providers to accept subsidies. Desperate not to lose the job she'd moved a twenty-plus-hour drive for, Aurora found a woman online who "wasn't doing childcare at the time. But she said she could take my son. But she did not take the [state assisted] payment. I didn't like it, I thought it was a weird situation, but I was so desperate; I was so desperate that I would lose the job." Aurora paid her out of pocket, which amounted to most of her new paycheck.

Voucher use also tends to be clustered in areas with lower average incomes adding to economic segregation. Some childcare providers in affluent areas are never even asked about accepting a subsidy. A study by the Urban Institute uncovered some troubling patterns among preschool providers who accepted vouchers, including lower teacher wages, higher teacher turnover, and more students assigned to each teacher. They found that half of family daycare providers and around 60 percent of daycare centers had served at least one student with a voucher in the previous six months. It's important to keep in mind, however, these rates are tracking the regulated childcare market, which doesn't include providers working off the books. According to the same report, one reason some providers cited for accepting students with subsidies was because of the guarantee of on-time payment for at least some part of the tuition.

Holding on to a childcare voucher is also tricky and usually short-lived. Poor moms navigate a tangle of rules and regulations in order to maintain their subsidies, and they cannot be late with their portion of the payment if they want to keep their spots. Losing a childcare voucher for even a month or two could mean dropping out of college for a semester or getting fired from a job because of excessive absences. The moms we spoke with worked around the clock to fulfill all of the requirements on a continuous basis, usually after long hours on the job and caring for kids.

A handful of mothers reported seeking advice from legal aid attorneys when their vouchers were terminated for paperwork errors, time limits, or problems with certification. Jennifer worried about losing her voucher when her cash assistance ran out. "Once she turns four, I have to be working full time because I've been on welfare for four years, you know? That is the cutoff," Jennifer said. So in the middle of her associate's degree program in nursing, which she enrolled in so she wouldn't "need these benefits anymore," her childcare voucher would be terminated. "The only way I can get my [childcare] voucher to stay is to work full time, forty hours a week. I mean I am going to school right in the middle of the day, so even if I go out and get a job it would have to be like three to eleven at night . . . then they'd only give me the voucher for three to eleven because they will only give me childcare if I'm working. So then I wouldn't have it during school, so I'm, like, screwed," she said. The attorney she consulted mentioned a possible loophole if she claimed to have a disability. "She [the lawyer] says because I go to counseling, anxiety and depression and stuff counts, but I'm, like, my counselor would be, like, 'she's fine,' you know? I mean it's just more stress trying to prove that I'm disabled when I'm not."

People often think that if you have a voucher, childcare is free, but this couldn't be further from the truth. You have to be working or looking for work to qualify for the voucher, and your income determines the amount of the subsidy (and the amount you still have to pay). The same is typically true of housing vouchers. "I hear people say, 'Oh, if you are on welfare, they will give you a voucher,' but no, that's not how it works," said Jamie, a mom of three with a baby on the way whom we met in chapter 4. Jamie was already struggling to pay for daycare for her toddler when she found out she was pregnant. "It is super expensive. I still pay a lot, a hundred-something per week, and that is with the voucher. He is a pre-schooler, so I think it would be $250 a week, and I pay half of that with the voucher," she said. When asked if her new baby would go to the same daycare, Jamie quickly responded. "No, it's almost $400 a week for an infant. . . . Before, it was a family voucher, but now it is an individual one, so every child has to go on the waiting list."

The average annual cost of daycare for an infant in the state of Massachusetts is a whopping $20,913, according to the Economic Policy Institute's childcare calculator, straining the budgets of even middle-class parents. A minimum-wage work-er would have to surrender their entire paycheck for more than ten months of the year to cover it. According to CLASP (the Center for Law and Social Policy), families below the poverty line who pay privately for childcare typically spend an aver-age of 30 percent of their income on it.[7] Rachel, a Black single mom to two boys in Boston, lost her childcare spot because she got so behind with the bills for after-school care for her seven-year-old son. At the time, she was working as a medical assistant and going to school to get her surgical technician cer-tification. "Because I owed the daycare so much, I said, okay, I am going to stop him going there until I can pay the whole bal-ance, because the more he is going, the bill becomes more and more, and I can't catch up, so that is what I did. And they said yes, so I did that, and I paid them in one month—I owed them eight hundred dollars. . . . But when I went back, they told me there is a new thing now with budget cuts, and you have to put your name on the [wait] list again." This after-school care, which made it possible for Rachel to go to school and work, was among the biggest bills in the household. Their rent in the public housing unit was income-adjusted, so according to Rachel, childcare, rent, and food ate up her entire paycheck, and when any small emergencies or even special occasions came up, she got behind. When her son was younger, Rachel had qualified for a childcare voucher, but, ironically, when he got older and only needed part-time care after school, she had to pay even more out of pocket.

The prohibitive cost of childcare forced several moms we met to compromise on the quality of care, just to ensure their kids were somewhere. Explaining the low-cost childcare option in her neighborhood, Jill said, "I grew up in the Polish Catholic Church, and so I knew a really inexpensive babysitter that's a family friend through there. She does catering and so she would be at home, and it was just the kind of thing you could bring your kid there for the day and it was super cheap, like thirty dollars for the day and convenient. She would watch a bunch of them, but it was like the TV was always on. She wasn't teaching them anything, but she's literally just watching them, feeding them, making sure they don't die. . . . Of course, I'd rather have [my daughter] somewhere else, learning, going out to the pool or the park if it was the summer. I didn't just want her stuck inside, but sometimes it wasn't worth it because I couldn't pay my other bills." There is no question that factors like cost and convenience impact poor mothers' decisions about childcare.

When her daughter turned four, Jill qualified for an income-adjusted preschool, which she and her daughter both love. "It's a sliding scale. I only pay $120 a week, and it's a longer, full day to five o'clock instead of three. When you first enroll, you have to show what you are making, and that's how they set our tuition," she explained. Jill appreciates that the teachers bundle up the kids and take them to play outside, no matter what the weather; the school is focused on learning and discipline, and it's only five minutes from her house. "It's the best childcare I've had so far, other than my parents."

Since Jill is currently between jobs, Amanda asked if she worried about the cost of tuition going up when she goes back to work. "No, they don't touch it once you're in the system. And I probably wouldn't tell them anyway," she answered, which makes sense in a world where jobs lack permanence. When you find an arrangement that works, you do everything you can to keep it.

Safety First

In California, Aurora's gamble to find childcare backfired, leaving her son in danger. She was nervous to drop her eight-year-old off so early in the morning with the woman she found online but didn't see any other option. "So I met up with her and that was on a Sunday and I was like, 'All right, Monday, I have to drop him off with the stranger, and at her home.' We did that for a few weeks," Aurora said. Then one day, she learned at work that her son was stranded at the bus stop. "I get a call from my eight-year-old . . . he is at this street corner and he calls me, and I'm on a job thirty minutes away. So I leave work to race over there to get him. I felt so much guilt; even though you did everything you could possibly think of doing, you feel terrible. They were so irresponsible." Later, she found out the childcare provider had gone on vacation and left her twenty-year-old son in charge. He forgot to pick up her son from the bus stop. "It was too much, too hard on him and me. I had to leave," said Aurora about her decision to leave the apprenticeship due to childcare crises.

Children's safety was the number one priority for the mothers we spoke with, and probably for most mothers across the country, regardless of income. For poor moms, though, fears about unsafe childcare lurked behind decisions about work and school. Many recalled terrifying past experiences when they had witnessed neglect and poor conditions. One childcare worker in Georgia described low-cost care in which kids were left in crowded, unclean, and unsafe conditions, including "roaches and broken toys and having no time to change them [diapers]." A mother in Denver reported that her child had been abused in a local daycare, and because of this, she would not send her other children to be cared for in childcare centers. Many of the moms indicated particular concern over poor conditions in daycare centers that accepted public vouchers. There were too many kids or too few teachers or buckets to catch water dripping from the ceiling. One mom in Denver explained that she had pulled her daughter out of a subsidized daycare after her complaints to the Colorado Childcare Assistance Program (CCAP) had gone unanswered. "I was afraid for her health. They didn't even change her diapers all day."

She removed her daughter from the center but was unable to find another placement, so she lost her job and was being evicted for nonpayment of rent.

Several mothers talked about how hard it was for childcare workers to provide good care, regardless of their commitment to children. Understaffed, often housed in an inadequate setting, with staff paid poverty wages, it is not surprising that staff turnover in the childcare field is among the highest in the nation. Research has shown how detrimental the churning of staff can be, but as many moms point out, it is a demanding job that is undervalued and underpaid.

In Connecticut, Jesse remembered working part time at a daycare center as a teenager. "I saw how badly they treated the kids. There were, like, too many babies in one room, it must have been illegal. They were not cleaning properly, and then I remember this one girl ended up puking and they put her in the closet for pickup, so the other parents didn't see her," she said. When asked if she thought this experience impacted her decisions about care for her daughter, Jesse answered right away: "It made me realize you don't know what's going on when you aren't there, and, like, not to trust it. Especially when they are too young to tell you what's going on. If it's not your kid, you are not going to treat them the same." Since Jesse was resolute about not leaving her daughter with strangers, she was thankful to have had family to support her daughter. "I have three 'babysitters'—my mom, my dad, and my grandma. So if I don't have one of them, I can't go, that's it." Jesse's reliance on family for childcare left her without options when the pandemic hit; they couldn't risk her grandmother's life, and so she lost another job.

Problems finding and keeping childcare wove in and out of the stories women told us, blocking them from moving up in work and school. In fact, 60 percent of parents in community conversations in Georgia said they lost a job due to problems with childcare. Roughly seven in ten women in the lowest-paid jobs in the United States are the breadwinners in their families, so job loss may be catastrophic. We heard countless stories of jobs lost and college credits and programs left half-earned. These mothers were not always fired or let go. Many left a job or dropped out of college because they could not find childcare that they could trust. "We need childcare so we can go to work and school and support our children. Unstable childcare is really terrible for them," acknowledged one mother in Denver. Her comment was met with vigorous nodding from around the table.

"I hid my daughter in the bottom of one of those big racks behind the bakery counter, but my boss found her. He saw her little feet hanging out," said Paula, a Latinx mom of three we met in chapter 2, describing a day when she had to go to work at ShopRite without childcare for her daughter. So she hid her five-year-old in the bread racks. "My boss was mad, but I told him I didn't have anywhere to put her, and he was really clear that I needed to be at work." Soon after, Paula left that job.

We heard from other moms who brought sick children with them to do homecare for disabled and elderly clients. Some mothers kept their children in cars in the parking lots of Walmart and Costco, running out on breaks to check on them. Others would leave a small child in the care of a somewhat older child for part of a work shift. And sometimes moms would sneak kids into the back of restaurants where they prepared food or motel rooms where they cleaned. Child-hiding practices are a way of life, we constantly heard. Some bosses colluded with moms hiding sick children, but if they got caught, everyone would have been in trouble—with a chain of authorities who could be notified starting with the restaurant owners and potentially moving on to the child welfare office and food safety officials. We listened to moms talk about how they operate in a gray zone in which everyone knows that there is no solution a parent can manufacture. They described all kinds of ways to try to keep an eye on a child when the larger society fails to provide a legitimate one. But it is understood that the default is always to blame low-wage parents, so to be a good mother they have to go underground.

In 2019, nearly a decade after the bread rack incident, Paula recalled her frustration searching for care for her kids while she worked "all these jobs" from McDonald's to ShopRite. Nobody at work, it seemed, had any regard for the well-being of her children. "I can laugh about it now, but at the time, it was a lot of stress . . . these managers are just about the bottom line. They are not thinking about the single moms working for them," she said. So when Paula found the position at Panera where she could take her kids to work and set them up in the café when there was a holiday or day off school, she desperately wanted to hold on to that job.

Childcare Outside the 9 to 5

Since the jobs available to low-income moms often come with unpredictable hours and little schedule control or flexibility, finding and maintaining consistent childcare arrangements may be impossible. Roughly 40 percent of American workers today have nonstandard hours, including night shifts, evenings, weekends, or rotating schedules; and these schedules are more common among low-wage workers.[8] Still, according to the most recent National Survey of Early Care and Education, 98 percent of daycare centers offer no evening hours and 94 percent no overnight options.

While most moms reported frustrated efforts to arrange childcare outside of the typical 9 to 5 workday, a few found twenty-four-hour daycare to be a lifesaving option. When Tea first moved to Portland, she took a job working from three to eleven and immediately went looking for care options for her then four-year-old daughter. "I was able to find twenty-four-hour daycare because of my schedule at that time . . . I didn't have a car. So I had to find a bus on the max line that was open till one o'clock in the morning. I would, you know, get off work and then get on the bus, then transfer and then pick her up at like 1 a.m. and get the last bus that ran to get to my apartment," she said. Finding overnight care allowed her to keep her job, but she and her daughter were still running around, sometimes in the middle of the night, to make it all work.

While very few moms we talked to were able to find subsidized nighttime care, many moms turned to family members and friends for help. Again, these equally wage-poor family members were left shouldering the burden when public benefit programs fell short. Aunts, uncles, and cousins would move in temporarily because they needed housing in exchange for helping out with childcare. Jill stayed living with her parents for the first three years of her daughter's life because "they were so helpful watching her, even though they were both working and, you know, we stayed in the same room. It was crowded. My brothers were also there at the time, but I couldn't afford to move out." Recently, she moved in with a roommate because "that's the only way we could afford the rent." Since her roommate is a longtime friend, she trusts him to watch her daughter occasionally if she needs some time out with her friends. "You know, I'll put her in her pajamas and get her in bed first, and she'll stay there. And you know, I trust him, he's my friend. He's really just there to make sure nobody robs us and she doesn't die, so it works." When asked how she would manage without help from friends and family, Jill said, "Honestly, I don't know how people do it." Similarly, Robin, a single mom of a ten-year-old son in Boston, said she was only able to go back to school in the evenings because her mom lived nearby and would "watch him in the evenings, because that's when my classes are. My mom will set him up with homework or take him to basketball, whatever he needs."

Stories like these reflect nationwide trends, with one in three kids in low-income families cared for regularly by relatives. Rates are even higher in families headed by single mothers. Relative care may foster bonds within the family and offer life-saving convenience, but too often the friend or family member doing the care is also low-income and managing their own difficult circumstances. Pam, a single mom of a six-year-old living in public housing in Boston, had to get to an early nursing class well before her daughter's school bus, so she relied on a neighbor for morning childcare. At the same time, she worried about relying on the neighbor, who she knew "had a lot of issues and things going on." Missing class in nursing school could have drastic consequences that Pam could ill afford, and yet she had no other option. Pam's daughter was lucky to have attended subsidized preschool and now had a spot in a high-quality magnet program with its own bus, even if her early morning childcare fell through. For many low-income kids, though, especially of preschool age, relative care takes the place of center or school-based care or preschool. Research shows this type of institutional care provides benefits like school readiness, socialization, and even higher wages later in life, not to mention reliability for parents trying to work and attend school themselves.[9]

Sandra, a single mom of three we met in chapter 2, counted on care from her roommate while she worked the overnight shift but hoped to find a more permanent childcare solution. "Occasionally, he [her roommate] will get mad and say, 'You are going to have to figure something out [find someone else to watch her kids overnight].'" Though she didn't think he would actually leave, the offhand threats made her nervous. And like many of the moms we spoke with, Sandra didn't have family living locally that could help out. As a teen, she was removed from her mother's care because of addiction and abuse. "I kind of fell out with my sister, and now she's not getting back to me. She doesn't have kids, so she doesn't really understand all that I'm going through." Later, Sandra was awarded temporary custody of her fourteen-year-old brother after he was removed from their mother's home. But then Sandra became homeless, and he went back to live with their mother. "It's too bad, because I know I could help him, and he could also help me watch the kids," she said.

To some professional parents, hiding kids in a bread rack or leaving them overnight or at five in the morning with a roommate or neighbor might seem like bad parenting. But for poor moms, these may be the best in a range of bad options. When living with your kids in the margins, subterfuge is often inevitable. Several mothers said they realized their chances of getting a job—even a minimum-wage job—were diminished by being a mom. This was a catch-22 for women across the country: you need to attend a meeting, get training, get a job, go to school in order to move your family out of poverty, but the unspoken assumption is you will be able to find someone to watch your kids while you do all these things. Parents told us they had no funds to pay a reliable babysitter even when they could find one. We listened to stories of children not being allowed at meetings and job training that was mandatory in order to qualify for public benefit programs.

Childcare in a Pandemic

When the pandemic hit, Sandra stopped sending her eighteen-month-old son to daycare, so she lost his voucher; school for her older kids went online. It felt too dangerous to send the kids anywhere and risk the exposure to COVID because of her older daughter's uncontrolled diabetes. "The kids are going really crazy. They haven't gone anywhere. We can't risk them getting sick, because when they get sick, it passes through the whole house," she said, recalling an incident the previous October when her older daughter got strep throat, spiked a 106-degree fever, and wound up in intensive care for two weeks. "I ended up getting fired for missing too many days," Sandra said.

In the fall of 2020, Sandra was scrambling to figure out how to handle the kids' seemingly never-ending remote schooling. Already, she feared she might lose her new overnight warehouse job at Lowe's. "It's always so hard finding jobs that work around the kids, but now that they are all homeschooling, it's impossible." When she gets home from work at 6 a.m., bone tired from working all night, it's time to set the kids up on their computers. "They just hate it, and I don't know what to do. I get them all ready, and then I leave to take care of the other one [her eighteen-month-old son], and my daughter will just be . . . not even doing it, or she'll just walk away." They live in a wooded area and always have problems with the internet signal dropping, so Sandra asked the school if they could prepare some printed packets for the girls. "Neither of them like it [online school], and it's a constant fight. I log them in and get them set up, and then they will just log themselves off. It's a lot of bullshit."

Like so many parents across the country, Sandra worries her kids' future will be jeopardized by pandemic schooling. "I just want them to finish school, and I want to make sure they never have to worry about being alone, like I was. Being close with each other and all that. They already talk about living in the dorms in college because they see that on YouTube, but I tell them they have to get good grades and scholarships." Sandra understands lots of kids across the country are struggling with learning from home. "These are desperate times, absolutely. The school psychiatrist has been trying to talk to a lot of kids—not just for remote learning—just because they miss being around their friends, teachers . . ."

Even in the next stage of the pandemic, with some kids returning in person to school, parents struggled to arrange care for their kids around suddenly unpredictable school and daycare schedules. Moms told us about dealing with shutdowns and quarantines in schools and daycares, which meant kids could have somewhere to go one week and then be back home the next, potentially upset and worried about an exposure. "You just can't plan, because you don't know what is going to happen with school. You know, I was going to go and look for a job, and then all of a sudden, I get a call from her school that they are going to shut all the way down again. So it's, like, okay, this is my job now. And there is no guarantee, even though now she's gone back, that it will stay open, so I would just have to quit a job," said Jesse.

There is no question that women, and single parents in particular, bore the brunt of the increase in childcare responsibilities during the shutdown. Four times as many women than men dropped out of the workforce and even more reported reduced hours and altered schedules.[10] What's more, single parents were more likely than married parents to lose their jobs and experience financial and material hardship in their households.[11] With family members and friends often now unwilling or unable to provide even occasional childcare, many single parents had no choice but to stay home. For most parents we spoke with, though, this was not a time for stress-free bonding with kids; record numbers of youth reported mental health struggles and difficulty managing anger and frustration.[12]

Self-Care Requires a Babysitter Too

Before the pandemic, Jamie was part of an empowerment program for single mothers in Boston, which focused on moving single parent–headed families out of poverty. She had recently finished up her bachelor's degree in human services, but with a baby on the way, she couldn't imagine going back to school and working without more childcare. "You also need childcare when you are searching for work or attending work training so we can do what we need to make our lives better. For our kids," said one mom in a Denver community conversation. Ironically, though, even some of the empowerment programs offered by local nonprofits failed to provide childcare during required meetings and functions.

Several women in interviews and community conversations expressed frustration about programs that required them to find "another babysitter" when they were already "working and at school during the week." Some preferred taking kids to meetings, even if that meant leaving them in on-site childcare. Colleen, single mom to five-year-old Joseph, couldn't believe the social mobility program she had joined didn't provide childcare during their required Saturday meetings. "They could reimburse or provide childcare on-site or something." Program staff, she said, urged participants to figure out their own childcare arrangements in an effort to adopt the culture of the professional world. Eventually, though, with attendance down at the meetings and moms voicing concerns, the program started to offer on-site care during meetings. Still, their initial reluctance shows that even professionals who work in human services with low-income families may not fully grasp what these moms face.

"Child care is a real barrier to Mom getting the help and services she needs, so you've got to have child care so that Mom can work on her own education and her own emotional support system," said Robert Monahan, the executive director of Julie's Family Learning Center in South Boston, a favorite program several moms mentioned to us. The philosophy at Julie's is to meet the needs of mom and child together. They call this a "total care" family approach, offering basic adult education, job and college counseling, tutoring for moms and kids, family counseling, and infant and toddler childcare with a Montessori preschool on-site.

While it makes sense to provide care for kids while helping moms, this type of integrative, two-generation approach to meeting the needs of family members together is not the norm even today. It was even more revolutionary when first imagined in the 1970s. Julie's was founded by Sister Jean Sullivan and Sister Louise Kearns, who were working with different populations in public housing projects in Boston. Sister Jean, a certified Montessori teacher, had started a preschool program for local kids. Meanwhile, Sister Louise was working with elementary school kids, realizing that when the moms are really struggling, it's hard to help the kids. The sisters talked while waiting to use a typewriter to apply for the same grant and decided to combine their applications. "They really were visionary women to be able to see that this would offer the families a much more holistic approach, combining the two loves," said Monahan. "They knew the kids needed help, and they knew the mothers were really struggling and wanted to learn how to be the best parents they could, but there were so many challenges."

"I feel very blessed to have him there," Colleen said about her son attending daycare and later preschool at Julie's. "There are only a few places in Southie that will take infants, and he's been there since he was five months old. And I went there along with him. That first year he was there in the infant room, I went there, and it was very therapeutic for me. Very supportive. I learned life skills, parenting skills." Staff later helped Colleen apply to an associate's degree program and get financial aid to attend a local community college.

In March of 2020, all of Julie's on-site services for moms and kids ground to a halt due to the pandemic. "It's been a real challenge to our model, you know, because most of our moms come here by subway, and our staff and moms and kids didn't feel safe. They weren't comfortable coming here, and really, how could we keep the required distance apart?" asked Monahan. Staff worked to connect over the phone, making sure moms had enough food, diapers, and wipes, as well as sanitizer, masks, and toilet paper, since many of these items were in short supply nationwide. They started to bring back moms and kids into the building in the fall by staggering cohorts, but then, in October, Boston public schools shut down, and they stopped offering on-site programming for the kids again, planning to restart during the spring of 2021. "We're all worried about regression with the children, especially with what they have experienced," said Monahan.

6

Moms and Kids on a Cliff

"I get my check back, and I cry. It's not enough for my children."

Atlanta, 2016

Dana: I worry every single day. My whole thing is how am I going to pay my rent every month? That's what I worry about every damn day that I go to work. And I do all of these crazy hours for the call center. I get my check back, and I cry. It's not enough for my children.

Cora: If they pay that low, why can't they just keep you on some public assistance when you're making some money?

Carmine: They don't *want* you to get ahead at all! They want to keep you down!

Brie: There are people that want to work. I don't want to live off the state. Why can't I make a little more, and be able to keep some?

Jennine: That's going to make a person self-sufficient.

Being able to have a little something for savings to fall back on.

Dana: It's impossible to save. Every time you make more money, they take more away.

Cora: The only thing you're left with is your kids looking at you, like, "What's going to happen?"

For working mothers, precariousness is the constant backdrop. Relying on public assistance to supplement poverty wages is like living on a cliff, because the foremost goal of those programs is to push your family off "the rolls." As Cora put it, your kids are with you on the cliff, and they turn to their mom for reassurance about "what's going to happen."

On a warm spring evening, we met with a group of eight mothers in a downtown Atlanta office building. The gathering included Black, white, and Latinx mothers. They didn't know each other, so we shared names on a sheet of flip-chart paper taped to the wall, and moms were eager to check out shared connections. One mother had worked with another's sister at a local call center, and they laughed as they shared stories of bizarre phone conversations and being monitored for "cheerfulness." As always, a couple of small children ran back and forth between the two rooms throughout the meeting, making sure their mothers had not disappeared. One mom holding a big baby on her lap passed him over to another mom who offered to give her arms a break.

Over the years, we found mothers were more open to talking about issues with public benefits and the "state" in these group settings, potentially because of the ugly stereotypes associated with public assistance. Moms invariably brought up their ongoing experiences with different benefits they used to supplement earnings that didn't cover the basics like rent, utilities, and food. They would commiserate with one another and offer advice, because holding on to any public aid is like walking a tightrope.

Welfare Moms: Racism and Misogyny at the Root

In the United States, racism is interwoven in the foundation of public assistance programs. First, families of color were systematically excluded from receiving public benefits, and then, with civil rights challenges leading to more equity at the welfare office, they were accused of being "welfare cheats." The programs are also driven by a particular kind of misogyny, a deep antipathy for single mothers who presumably have babies carelessly and then live off hardworking (white) folks. A 2021 report by the Center on Policy and Budget Priorities examines the way welfare policies reflect a history of racism.[1] Ife Floyd, a report co-author, explained to New Jersey Advanced Media, "Those narratives are really critical in persuading policy makers to tell a story that these Black and Brown people have a lot of kids, they're lazy, and they're just living off the dole. That's what was being peddled."

This long-standing distortion of poor motherhood lives on in the public imagination. It is reflected in every program designed for poor women and children. The very name of the major policy shift—the 1996 welfare reform legislation called the Personal Responsibility and Work Opportunity Reconciliation Act (PRWRA)—reflects the assumption that poor moms need tough regulation to become responsible and get a job. Rhetoric from both Democrat and Republican lawmakers proclaimed that ending welfare benefits would promote the "dignity of work." Yet all of these proponents overlooked years of data that most welfare-reliant mothers already had extensive work histories. They moved in and out of low-paid jobs based on their children's needs and unstable labor market demands. But the "welfare mom" stereotype is tenacious, hanging on even as mothers enter the labor force and remain there for years. It also justifies a level of policing and punishment that cannot be found in other social assistance programs such as Social Security, small business loans, veterans benefits, subsidies through tax breaks, or interest-free loans to corporations. Even today, several states continue to employ family or child cap policies when distributing Temporary Assistance for Needy Families (TANF) or cash welfare benefits. The reasoning: if poor women stop receiving an increase in TANF benefits when they have another child, they will stop having children. In recent years, states like Massachusetts and New Jersey have repealed their family cap laws as studies have shown that these laws do not decrease births, but do, in fact, increase hardships for families.[2]

What we heard most from moms who were juggling public assistance and jobs was that welfare rules are a minefield. Alongside the hyper-scrutiny of poor mothers, their families never received more than scant aid and jumped through numerous hoops to get it. Over the years, women from different states described a system that was bent on catching them, obsessed with discovering liars and cheaters. It is not, Carmine and other mothers in Georgia explained, a social welfare system that is seeking to advance poor families by, for example, investing in mothers' higher education and providing children with high-quality preschool. Most of the women described domestic programs for the working poor as designed "to keep you down."

The Cliff Threat

Beyond incoherence and misinformation, a universal issue facing families receiving public assistance is the constant threat of losing it. Referred to as "cliff effects," this is the sudden and often unanticipated decrease in some or all of assistance that mitigates income poverty. The loss can be one program or many, including food aid, health care, child nutrition programs, housing aid, and childcare. It can lead to homelessness. This cliff was a haunting presence among parents we talked to across the nation. If you cross an income eligibility line, it's like dominoes, they said. First, losing eligibility for subsidized childcare, for example, and then losing employment because you can't leave kids alone, and then—worst of all—with no pay, facing the nightmare of eviction. Parents described constant vigilance about how close they were to that edge and told us how this fear controlled every decision they made. Jana, a mother in Atlanta, was one of several women who "turned down a raise" in the restaurant where she was employed. She knew that it would nudge her income just over the line, and a small wage increase would mean a far larger loss in food aid (SNAP benefits). But she worried that turning down a raise feeds into a degraded image of poor moms: "It makes you seem like you *want* to stay on welfare."

Atlanta, 2016

Dana: Yeah, so, like, the cliff effect. Like for my housing, if my portion of what I can pay goes over $598, then I no longer qualify for that unit. If I make $599 a month, then they'll take away my rent voucher. Now I can't get anything. Because if I can pay $599, does that mean I can go get an apartment for $1,500 bucks a month, right? And then, I just got into low-income childcare. But then they just took my food stamps from $397 to $22 per month. So that's another thing . . . I do seasonal work so my hours are really variable. I'm going to be working more in the springtime. So they calculate what you're earning, but they calculate based on the last month.

Jennine: I can't believe they had the nerve to give you $22. I get $36 of food stamps. I literally tried to give it back. I'm, like, "Give it to someone else." We're talking about how we're broke and budget cuts and all. Just give it to someone else. "No we can't do that." It's $36. What am I supposed to do with that?

Dana: They miscalculated my income by $1,000. They said I was making a thousand more a month than I was. I was, like, "This is a mistake. This is the paperwork I gave you. This is the math of what I gave you." I said this is a mistake. And they said, "Well, you're going to have to talk to somebody about that." You can go wait in line for three hours. So I didn't have time to wait three hours to get it sorted out. Now,

> what they want me to do is to recertify every month
> (a technique to hyper-regulate a parent). And then
> they'll calculate what they're going to give me based
> off of the last month that I turned it in. I'm all on my
> own; we all are.

Many welfare policy analysts agree with these moms. Randy Albelda and Susan Crandall, leading social welfare researchers at the University of Massachusetts, point out that small wage increases do not come close to making up for the loss of food stamps, childcare, or other benefits designed to help people living in or near poverty. Small gains that could gradually stabilize a family become grounds for pulling out the rug.[3] These tiny incremental gains are all that low-wage jobs ever offer their workers. But parents have learned they can ultimately be harmful to their families' stability and safety. So we heard how mothers will turn down a raise, more hours of work, or a better position offered because of their hard work. Moms like Jana, who told us about refusing a raise, understand that a small raise of even fifty dollars a week might be taken back threefold in lost benefits. She also understands that other people could misinterpret turning down a raise, because on its face it seems to say, "'No, I don't want the raise.' Who says that?"

A Twisted System Grows Up

Every parent we met loathed communicating with or visiting public assistance offices, but they told us they had no choice. Of all the working moms who took part in the community conversations, three-quarters were eligible for some form of assistance based on income poverty. They described the system as a convoluted, obstructive bureaucracy that many believed was designed to find a way to deny aid. An African American mom in Atlanta said, "The whole system sets people up to fail." Nodding, an older white woman who was raising her grandchildren agreed. "It punishes people who are trying to do better" through work, additional education, or training efforts. Welfare reform made it much more difficult for mothers receiving public assistance to attend college. Though programs vary by state, welfare reform created a system that no longer counted hours spent in school as "work," limited the time welfare recipients could devote to education, and established rules around allowable types of training and education. As a result, researchers report decreases in the likelihood of college enrollment of welfare recipients ranging between 20 and 80 percent.[4] So it should not come as a surprise that mothers across the country described public assistance as a system designed not to help them move ahead but instead to control and thwart their efforts.

This approach to poverty programs has deep roots in the United States. Historically, welfare was largely understood to be a substitute for white male wages due to the death, absence, or unemployment of husbands/fathers. Intended for white widows and then increasingly for divorced or "abandoned" mothers with children, the absence of a "man in the house" was the justification for helping poor white families. But by the latter part of the twentieth century, civil rights challenges to largely white-only safety nets meant that Black and Brown families started gaining access to welfare benefits. These families had long been disproportionately poor, and so, as they claimed a

larger share of the "welfare rolls," the nation's simmering racist attitudes emerged.

During this same period, middle-class and affluent mothers
were increasingly entering the labor force, often purchasing
the labor of poor women to substitute for them in the home.
Two-career families began to emerge as the new normal.
Though concentrated among the professional and affluent
class, this became a dominant version of family life, juxta-
posed with poor families that needed aid so moms could be
available to care for kids. Also during these decades, many
more women—white, Black, and Brown—were having children on their own. As depicted by white conservative male
voices, single moms became the face of the erosion of the
nuclear family model. Families headed by single mothers had
high rates of poverty and were disproportionately Black and
Brown, along with millions of white families. By 1994, the
core welfare program, Aid to Families with Dependent Children (AFDC), saw caseloads peak with 14.2 million recipients in over 5 million families. Two-thirds of these recipients
were children. Armed with evidence of the alarming increase
in welfare use associated with single motherhood, "welfare
moms" became the nation's ruling social problem. And the
primary bipartisan explanation was that poor women were
having babies irresponsibly. The problem wasn't that the jobs
they could get paid only poverty wages. And it wasn't that the
United States lagged behind all other developed nations in providing supports like childcare to stabilize low-income families.
The problem was the women.

Welfare mothers became a national obsession, with both
Democrats and Republicans piling on. Rhetoric from that

time suggested that mothers getting public assistance had "dependency" problems and even were "addicted to welfare." The only solution was to cut them off. Ronald Reagan, U.S. president in the late 1980s, popularized the term "welfare queen" and galvanized anti-welfare sentiments. He articulated the central mission of public assistance for poor families: "We should measure welfare's success by how many people leave...." with no mention of whether or not they had escaped poverty. Within a few years after welfare reform was enacted, the number of children and mothers receiving public assistance tumbled by 60 percent. While in 1979 over 80 percent of poor families were receiving AFDC, ten years after welfare reform that had dropped to 27 percent as hundreds of thousands of mothers were forced into the nation's lowest wage and most unstable labor markets.[5]

Welfare reform succeeded in eliminating families from the caseload, yet researchers found that instances of deep poverty actually increased. What's more, poor families across the country still report needing help, but now they are much less likely to receive it.[6] Years later, the evidence continued to mount that while families might see more dollars in earnings each month than they received from public assistance, they were also facing many more costs.

A Brookings Institution report showed that it is not jobs or social programs that keep poor moms afloat; rather, family members, likely also low-income, provided more support than wages and public assistance.[7] We also found this to be the case. We heard dozens of stories of working poor family members trying to help a struggling sister or daughter or aunt who was raising children on poverty incomes. The gap caused by welfare reform is most often covered by the poor people themselves, stretching to survive.

Given how little moms earn and, inevitably, how low-income their kin are too, they continue to need public assistance even when employed. This was true for most of the parents we met over the years. Of 130 families from which we collected specific economic information, annual incomes ranged from $10,000 to $44,000, with more than half of incomes under $28,000. In the cities where we held community conversations—Denver, Atlanta, and Boston—we compared incomes of the women who attended with the national estimates of what families need to cover the basics, using the EPI Family Budget Calculator, which accounts for housing costs, food, childcare, health insurance, transportation, and other necessities such as a cell phone, heat, electricity, clothing for growing children, car seats for babies, tampons, and diapers. As we illustrated in chapter 2, the income needed to meet basic needs for Lenore, living in Denver with her two kids, would be $89,533. In Atlanta, where costs of living are lower, the same family would require about $68,000. In Boston, a very expensive city, that family would need $103,000 to cover basic costs. Comparing these with the incomes of the parents we met, mothers were earning less than a third to about one-half of what experts calculated as a budget that would meet basic family needs.

Lenore was living with her sister in Denver after escaping domestic abuse. She earned about $450 a week from her two part-time jobs. She received SNAP benefits to subsidize food costs and was careful to be sure her earnings did not fluctuate and jeopardize that subsidy. Between work shifts, Lenore went to the local Goodwill and churches for clothing and to food pantries to stretch her SNAP benefits. But her greatest need was to find her own place to live, not only because the two families were crowded and she was overstaying her welcome with her sister. Most pressing, Lenore was jeopardizing her sister's subsidized housing. "We aren't supposed to have three kids where we are. I know we should get our own place. How do I save? I don't make my bills now," she said.

Her sister's subsidized apartment came with rules. This is common. Low-income people who get public assistance in the form of rent subsidies must abide by strict regulations, one of which is not allowing others, including needy family members, to move in with them. Despite that, Lenore's sister was a family member who—as researchers noted—was more critical for Lenore's family than jobs or public assistance, stepping in to help at risk to her own family. The two sisters were flying under the radar. Lenore would tell the kids to be very quiet so the neighbors wouldn't find out about, or at least be bothered by, the doubled-up household. This meant keeping the children busy after school and away from the apartment when they were energetic and playful. In between jobs and on weekends, she would try to tire them out before setting them up in front of a screen and leaving for her second job in the evenings. How tired was *she* by that time of the day? "I was always exhausted," Lenore said.

Denver, 2016

> **Briana:** It's difficult to navigate the systems. I think they do that so you won't apply for those [public assistance] programs.

Deb: But if you're persistent and if you can get through everything . . .

Amy: But yeah, it's like a part-time job.

Deb: And sometimes they treat you terribly, but there is a helpful component to it too; without SNAP you wouldn't be able to feed your children, without Medicaid you wouldn't have health care.

Christy: My issue is that I wanted to get my daughter into this preschool, and I had to fill out childcare paperwork. But in order to do that I'd need to put my baby's daddy on child support. Either I put my baby's daddy on child support or pay $200 more a month. He's in jail. He's not about child support, and he hasn't got a job. So, I had to start paying child support, because I didn't want to put my baby's daddy on child support. Why am I paying child support if I'm taking care of my kids? They want you to boo-hoo cry in front of them, break down, and show all of these police reports [about previous domestic violence].

Amy: You're being retraumatized.

Christy: I'm in fear; I cannot reach out to them. [Christy was afraid if she gave them too much information her abusive ex-spouse would find her.]

Amy: That can be retraumatizing. I was working for a month part-time minimum wage and they reduced my food stamps and took away my TANF, so now I have to show how much I'm paying in rent because my rent went up as well. They said I was earning all that much, *but it was only for a month.*

In all of the places we went, parents described seeking state aid as another job, one that had to be crammed into already stressful working-family lives. In setting dates for appointments, most state authorities ignored moms' precarious schedules juggling jobs and children. One mom recounted her experience trying to sign up for cash assistance, which required a mandatory intake class that was scheduled at the same time as another class she was also required to attend (across town) in order to keep her childcare voucher. Public assistance program staff are not required to talk to one another—that is left to moms. Parents said that whenever "they" tell you to show up, you do, and whatever requirements they dictate, you must perform their script. You have to or "you lose everything."

Moms explained you can't count on compassion from caseworkers or state officials because they hold all the cards. The impact of this stressful and unpredictable system is absent from policy research that evaluates social welfare programs. Program success is measured by closing cases, no matter how they end and what happens to those families. Moms said they were never asked how their family was faring or how their kids were doing in school. Instead, they were grilled endlessly to uncover flaws in their eligibility, any cash gifts they might have been given, any off-the-books income, any adjustment to their tiny family budgets that would justify reducing the aid they received or cutting them off entirely.

Recounting their experiences applying for and receiving government assistance, most parents described long and

incoherent processes designed to "make you give up." It starts
with interviews, in person and online, to determine income
eligibility. If a mom makes it through that gate, then there is
the wait, sometimes for many weeks, while trying to keep a
family afloat and intact. The next communication is finding
out the level of "allowable aid." Sometimes it is a pittance. We
heard many stories from low-wage moms putting in maximum
effort to only receive tiny subsidies, like Dana in Georgia, who
had been running out of food halfway through the month on
her minimum wage retail paycheck. After jumping through
numerous hoops to apply for food assistance, she was allotted
$20 a month in SNAP benefits, which she realized "was not
even worth the effort."

Once they are granted some amount of food aid or hours
of childcare or other assistance, the demands keep coming.
In order to retain eligibility, moms must attend meetings,
often during work hours. Sometimes new paperwork would
be required that, with no previous notice, parents might not
have with them for a scheduled meeting, which could turn into
grounds for potential termination of benefits. College students
who managed to qualify for welfare benefits told us about
the never-ending requirements for signatures from professors
and documentation of time spent in labs and studying, which
was difficult and time-consuming to produce, not to mention "humiliating to ask for." Universally, we heard that you
seldom meet the same state official, so again and again you
must explain yourself, your job demands, rent changes, earnings that often change, children's needs, and why getting some
assistance is justified.

"It's a twisted loop," said Jennine, a white mother in her
forties. "It's a system of no continuity. It hurts everybody. You

do the right thing; you don't get anything." Another mother agreed, adding that the problem is the state doesn't actually look at take-home pay, which may vary wildly week to week, or student debt or other bills. "I'm sure if they did, they'd see that I have zero frickin' dollars," she said, and several mothers nodded around the table. Then Jennine added, "I've had periods too where I'm starting to make a little bit more money, but I have to limit my hours at work because if I work a little bit more, I lose everything [all the benefits she relies on]." An image emerged from the community conversations of a culture of seemingly intentional misinformation. You might go into a state office one day and be told you need to produce additional documents and then, upon returning, meet with a different person who dismisses the papers you just took time off work to obtain. After journeying through this convoluted maze, moms might then be told that some paperwork has been misplaced and needs to be resubmitted. Invariably, when mistakes were made, the outcome was the loss of time and resources for the low-income family.

Multiple reviews, new demands, misinformation, and lost paperwork were ubiquitous even with the expansion of electronic data management. But what moms found most outrageous in these encounters was that invariably *they* had to solve the problem. It was up to them to remedy all issues, to return to the office at another date, resubmit papers, or get a new form or verification of bills, wages, and so forth. This was the case even when the mistake was not theirs. It was on moms to resolve everything because their family was at stake. They understood this as signaling the "state" attitude that they were unimportant. Colette, a Black grandmother in Boston, raised a challenge. "Do you think they'd treat some white guy, who owes back taxes, like this? I worked for someone who had to work out a plan. He'd skipped his taxes for three years. They sat down with him and worked out a plan, so he could pay it back." She went on to point out that this former boss was a known cheater who had intentionally broken the law. But low-wage mothers needing public assistance are routinely interrogated like criminals, just because they are poor and need help.

Essie, a single mom from Boston, recounted a story about the state finding an error in its own calculations that refunded her $1,312 in food stamps but, because of that, the state demanded she pay back $1,000 to TANF. "Well, it was your mistake," she said. "The penalty part is kind of ironic. What is their agenda behind trying to fine someone who clearly has no money in the first place? You fill out every paper. You fill out every form. You jumped through every hoop and then it's somehow your fault?" In response, Colette advised the parents to always keep a file of original documents "in your bag, with you whenever you go [to the state offices] and *never* give them over." If the state official wants the papers, "tell her to make a copy right then, and if she can't," do not leave them, because they will get lost. Colette warned the group, "You have to take back some control." She went on to critique the language that Lisa and the research team used on that day when they asked the group about experiences with "public assistance." She said, "It's not assistance; I don't call it that. I call it public control."

We heard repeatedly a suspicion that the piling-on of changeable demands was intended to encourage mistakes or serve as a deterrent to the receipt of assistance, a way to "just wear us out." One mom, working part time as a security guard at night and as a homecare worker by day, was still earning so little that she was eligible for several public benefits in Massachusetts. But they made it impossible for her to comply with their regulatory demands. She remarked, "We have to come up with our own hustles on the side because they make it impossible." Yet the under-the-table "hustles," moms know, also put them at risk if they are caught and feed the image of welfare cheats. Another woman emphasized this point. She said, "They make it so you have to lie."

Rooting Out the Cheats

Today, the national obsession with finding poor parents who "cheat the system" continues to dominate the design of public assistance programs. Of course, other fraud consumes far more taxpayer money—for example, billions in inflated prices paid to defense contractors and to cover fraudulent claims to Medicare. The 2020 fiscal year estimate for improper payments for claims paid by Medicare was 6.27 percent, which represents $25.74 billion.[8] But the actors in these thefts are often wealthy defense contractors or networks of corporations providing health services, not poor parents. In a description of "inaccuracy and misconduct" in an analysis of food stamps use, the culprits included retailers who abuse the sale of food stamps, state agency errors, and misuse by low-income recipients. Nonetheless, it is these recipients who have become the face of food stamp cheating, though they comprise a tiny percentage of the total cost. The term used for poor mothers' misuse of food stamps is to say they are "trafficking" them, calling to mind extreme criminality. But, as moms explained to us, there are critical products you cannot buy with food stamps. For example, a survey of low-income women in 2019 found that "nearly two-thirds couldn't afford menstrual hygiene products such as tampons or pads during the previous year."[9] This turns out to be a common reason for some women "trafficking" food stamps, because they are swapping them for tampons, diapers, and toothpaste. Otherwise, they explained, they must resort to using "toilet paper, paper towels, and newspapers" when menstruating or diapering babies.

The abuse of social programs by poor people routinely makes headlines. "The Great Food Stamp Binge," for example, is a Fox News documentary that strings together sensational accounts of people who don't actually need food assistance but are "taking millions from the government" in the form of free food. While food stamp fraud may be the most popular in the media, we also heard about housing investigations. In several cases, state regulators turned into investigators, trying to catch recipients cheating the system. Parents in Massachusetts described how their families were "investigated" when they applied for help, particularly housing aid. In one case, Glendora, at the time a recently evicted mother, said her brother had allowed her family to double up with his family until she was approved for a shelter. She described how someone came by one day and "knocked on his door" to look over his home. They were investigating whether she actually needed shelter or was cheating the system. Her brother had offered short-term access to a couch and floor to his sister and her two children, and now he was forced to allow them to enter and show the constrained housing, the number of children, and living quarters. He explained that despite the overcrowding, he wanted to keep his nephews out of foster care and his sister from homelessness. Glendora was humiliated by the way her housing crisis forced her brother to "explain himself" as though he was conspiring in fraud. Glendora asked the other mothers, "Why would you help your family if that's what happens?"

Annette, a grandmother in Georgia, offered a similar story. She had taken in her granddaughter to protect her from an "abusive situation," wanting to provide the teenage girl with some structure that had been lacking in her previous chaotic household. Annette helped her find an after-school job and encouraged her to keep her grades up. But when they realized that the girl's income, added to her grandmother's part-time earnings and her great-grandfather's disability pension, pushed the household over the income limit and caused them to lose more in food and rental aid, Annette had to tell her granddaughter to quit. "What kind of message is that?" she asked the group. Arlette, also in Boston, informally adopted two grandchildren years before, but was still afraid to go through the process of formal guardianship. A family advocate in a local community center had pointed out that she would receive state help in raising the children, but life had taught her that any change in her income could trigger the cascade of losses, and above all, she was frightened about losing housing, the worst nightmare for low-income families.

A New Wave of Anti-welfarism

While early in the pandemic COVID was called "the great equalizer," that assessment quickly foundered as it became clear that race and class were major factors, not only in who got sick, but who got treatment, vaccinations, and help to recover. Many media outlets reported how the virus was exposing long-existing inequalities. Talking to working poor parents, many of them Black and Brown, they suggested this "exposure" of inequality was predictable. "I could have told them who was going to suffer the most," a labor organizer for low-income service workers told us. But beyond who was getting sick and who was getting protective equipment, it was who was getting the benefit of bailout funds and "paycheck protection" that exposed another long-standing disparity. While some moms worked in "essential" jobs, and so were expected to be at work, without childcare, many had to cut back or quit. Parents working in hospitality, food, and retail were let go in droves and many did not benefit from any paycheck protection. Only two of the moms we met had the option of virtual work; for most, their bodies were the basis of their jobs serving, cleaning, aiding, and caring for people.

Shalaya pointed out that if anyone *"had just asked,"* long before a pandemic, she and her sister and millions of other parents would have pointed out all the ways that they are routinely blocked from any recovery from disruption and trauma. They disclosed survival strategies low-income moms have long used—trading a few food stamps for tampons, giving family members sanctuary from domestic violence despite the housing rules, hiding kids at work when childcare arrangements fall through, working a job under the table to offset poverty wages—all of which could be held against you during a national crisis. Danielle, a Connecticut mom and Shop-Rite cashier, and her fiancé were too afraid to go through with his claim for unemployment after he was forced to leave his job to care for their kids full time during the shutdown. They needed the extra income, but feared if they got some money and then "the rules changed, they could, you know, take it back later when we don't even have it." Low-income families, particularly BIPOC and immigrant families, share a history of being punished for some unknown infraction after they have received aid and being left to deal with the fallout.

But for some families, the "rescue package" direct payments were lifesavers, especially for those who would not qualify for loans. Throughout 2020 and 2021, we heard about how the monthly checks that people were receiving from the federal government meant they could cover bills, hold on to apartments, and take care of kids who had become homebound with schools or daycares closed. Receiving a cash influx or having rent payments put off meant the chance to care for children amid the shutdown. According to some, this was the only reason they could keep their families intact. The supplemental employment support has been particularly helpful for single moms who are home with their children, but it has become a scourge to pro-business, anti-welfare interests.

As of this writing, infection rates have declined and businesses are opening up; a demand for cheap labor is back and the low-paid labor market has become very tight. In many cases, businesses have been unable to hire back enough cheap labor to stay up and running. Rather than raise wages and benefits to attract workers in a competitive labor market, some Republican lawmakers sought to end the rescue checks that had made it possible for low-income families to get by. Professor Katz at the University of Houston reflected on the media focus on businesses not being able to hire enough workers. "I wonder about the way the media and the Right are running the narrative about employers having trouble hiring people at, like, $7.25 an hour to do this work. I would say shitty jobs that don't have any respect, that have awful hours, that are very hard work. So people would rather stay home on unemployment. It's being framed as a problem for the workers, instead of us looking at it from a societal frame and saying, 'Well, why do we allow employers to exploit low-wage workers in that way?' If you are getting unemployment, and your body is able to heal some from years of a bad low-wage job, and you're spending time with your kids, and you're keeping yourself safe from the virus, why wouldn't you do that?"

One tactic lawmakers used to gain support for ending pandemic benefits for mothers and children came right out of the anti-welfare playbook. Florida congressman Greg Steube beat that old drum: "Democrats chose to turn our nation into a welfare state with more government handouts." John Kabateck, former executive director of the National Federation of Independent Business, used the welfare mother trope to support cutting family benefits: "It will be a matter of time before showing up for work is a better-paying proposition than remaining on the couch watching reruns of *Gilligan's Island*." By June of 2021, twenty-five states were refusing the $300 supplemental unemployment benefits and some were also ceasing participation in other pandemic-related unemployment benefits. The underlying goal: remove any choice from working people who fill the lowest rungs of the labor market. The same voices lobbying for ending unemployment aid simultaneously worked to block investment in childcare proposed by the Biden administration. Tennessee senator Marsha Blackburn argued in a Fox Business Network interview that new childcare proposals would "incentivize women to rely on the federal government to organize their lives," resonating with the same degrading stereotype of the dysfunctional welfare mother.

The only constant for low-income families looking for help from the state is instability. An administration led by a Democratic president may loosen up eligibility rules and increase benefits. It may, as the Biden administration is trying to do, infuse a significant increase in food, childcare, and rental subsidies in the wake of the pandemic. But should a new Republican administration roll into town, these gains in stability could dissipate in months. And as evidenced by the Clinton administration's passage of welfare reform, Democrats do not always expand social programs for the poor. Cycles of losses and new restrictions ripple through low-income communities, particularly affecting BIPOC communities that often have a higher percentage of low-income families. At the kitchen table of working poor families, moms have to constantly revise their formula as well, trying to juggle low wages with little pots of public assistance while still not making ends meet. "My two-year-old tries to share her food with me," a mom named Patrice recalled. "My two-year-old comes up to me and says, 'Okay, okay.' That's all she knows how to say to me when I'm sad. It's not right for her. Nobody sees what goes on behind closed doors."

7

Keeping Us in Our Place

"I watched my mother and my grandmother keep trying to get ahead. My mother had me when she was fifteen, and so they really raised me together. They kept going back to this education program or that one. My grandmother went back to college in her fifties. So, it was always stuck in my mind that I had to keep at education."

Linda was twenty-seven in 2016 when she met Lisa at a café close to the urban university campus where she was completing her undergraduate degree. An African American mother of two small boys, Linda talked about finishing up coursework for a degree in "pre-med or pre-pharmacology." At the time, she described juggling the needs of her three- and five-year-old sons with her classes and part-time job; it sounded overwhelming. "You have to work the schedule with all three [college, job, and children]. They don't want to hear about the other." The childcare center staff, Linda said, were incredibly helpful. They knew about the rules of the state's childcare program. They understood the razor's edge a mom walks, satisfying the work requirement hours but keeping income low enough not to be knocked out of eligibility because you earn too much. They knew about the grade level and number of credit hours you have to keep up too, in order to continue to be eligible for childcare assistance. They helped Linda patch together enough hours of required class time, work time, and, when possible, a little extra study time before she headed home to care for her sons.

Before she entered college, already a single mom, Linda said she'd been recruited into "sham certificate programs," first to service sound equipment and then to become a medical assistant. This experience was not unique; many of the moms we interviewed had "certificates to nowhere," as Anna, a thirty-eight-year-old white mother of two, put it. Anna had finally entered college after being encouraged by her state "self-sufficiency coach" to go through several training programs that left her jobless, without prospects, and in debt.

"No one looks out for you. It's a sham, they take your money, you take these bullshit classes, and you have a piece of paper that means nothing." In Linda's view, there is a whole industry feeding on desperate people. While her mother and grandmother encouraged education, they did not know how to advise Linda about avoiding predatory for-profit education and training programs. This is a challenge for anyone not well versed in navigating pathways through higher education, trade, or technology programs that would lead to a family-supporting income. In fact, Betsy DeVos, the U.S. secretary of education from 2017 to 2021, did her utmost to open season on vulnerable people seeking social mobility or, as Marc Egan from the National Education Association put it, to help "these predatory institutions" exploit the vulnerable, "including veterans, older students, students of color, disabled students, and students who are the first in their families to attend college." Linda thinks that if the children of affluent families were sent to these bogus programs, the businesses would be sued and then dismantled. But as long as they are feeding off poor and working-class people, there are few protections and little uproar.

The second time Lisa got together with Linda, she brought her little boys along. It was a hot day, and they walked down to the city riverfront so the boys could play in a fountain that spurted water from jets at varying angles. Marcus held his little brother's hand as they crouched, waiting for the rush of water, shrieking as it spurted up. They glanced over to their mother, who smiled at them.

On this day, Linda went deeper into her history. "I left home when my mother married my stepfather. I had conflicts with him." She had been an honors student in high school but dropped out, moved out, and eventually ended up homeless and pregnant. Her partner, struggling with alcoholism, had moved on. At that point, her mother—separated from her spouse—and her grandmother reclaimed Linda and her baby. Two years later, when she started dating the father of her younger son, Jerod, her mother and grandmother took in her partner as well, deciding he was a good man. Still, Linda was reluctant to marry, even though her current partner was an employed carpenter and dedicated father who helped pay the bills. "He is a good dad. I trust him a lot. But I told him we have to wait for a while longer. At least I want to finish this degree."

Linda talked about losing time after Jerod was born. "I had postpartum anxiety with my second. I needed help to get through, and that's what I want to do [in her career]." That day in the sun, with her little boys running over to spray her with droplets of water, Linda told Lisa she had decided to pursue a nurse practitioner degree to focus on helping new moms.

Lisa: How hard is it to juggle your boys and keep going with college and everything?

Linda: I think about it every day. If it's late, and I've been in classes, gone to work, come home, and put the boys to bed, I don't want to do an assignment. I want to sleep. But I think about them. They keep me going. They will go to college.

Lisa: You're sure of that?

Linda: (Laughing) Oh honey, they do not have an option, and they already know it.

Lisa: What would make a difference for you and other moms, trying to move up?

Linda: *Do they even want us to get through?* We have kids, we need childcare. *Do they get that?* It's like you have to work at these jobs that pay nothing, so you can get childcare, so you can go to classes. Why? Do any of them [politicians, professors, and policy makers] expect their kids to do all that? We need financial aid that takes children into account. They have to stop looking down on people who have kids.

Who Gets to Get Ahead?

Social mobility is the sacred narrative of the United States. It is a tale celebrating economic gain and individualism as the root of the American character. It is a revered version of the nation that systematically excludes and distorts the women we met. Fed by entrenched racism, disdain for poor people and their children, and widespread misogyny, the dominant narrative has long stereotyped poor mothers as dependent and immoral. We listened to hundreds of wage-poor women describe their lives and within that collective account, they spoke back to this version of their identity. They pointed out the blockades they face at every turn, from girlhood to grand-mothering, that reflect the nation's denigration of poor mothers. They also raised a missing history about how working poor, often single, moms, many of whom are women of color, have always rejected malignant stereotypes about how they live and persist.

As the previous chapters reflect, we gathered hundreds of accounts of demanding girlhoods, poverty-pay jobs, state aid going AWOL, and chronic family-care crises. We also learned about extraordinary efforts of moms from all over the country, women from diverse race and ethnic backgrounds, trying to break out of the wage-poverty trap. We met a few who had gone into hard military service solely because it offered education and health benefits. We heard from women devoting countless hours to numerous certificate programs, most of which took up time and money and did not provide a living wage. The two exit plans we heard about most were efforts to get a college degree and trying to apprentice into decent-paying trade jobs. Threaded throughout these diverse narratives was the story of persistence that dominates these women's lives. They kept on climbing despite every obstacle thrown in front of them and despite all the responsibility that they carried.

The Invisibility of Moms in College

Linda's questioning of the sincerity of those in power to help working poor moms reflects national research on student parents. The Institute for Women's Policy Research (IWPR) points to a general lack of research on college students who are raising children, despite the fact that more than one in five undergraduates is a parent, and more than 70 percent of student parents are mothers.[1] Sixty-two percent of those are single mothers. This part of the college student population just isn't a priority for the vast majority of institutions of higher education who continue to focus attention and resources on dwindling numbers of straight-from-high-school coeds supported by their parents. Even the well-documented evidence that mothers' pursuit of higher education will encourage their children to do the same—as Linda put it, her little boys already understand that they *will* go to college—hasn't led to much interest or investment in low-income parents' college success. This lack of support has real impacts: only around 4 percent of parenting undergraduate students attain a degree within six years of enrollment.[2] What's more, women who are Black, Latinx, indigenous, and first-generation immigrants are the most likely to be mothering while attending college, so the impact is outsized in communities of color. Their families— and therefore BIPOC communities in general—are disproportionately harmed by the lack of support for parents who are trying to do better by getting a college degree.

Many of the women we spoke with expressed the desire for themselves and their children to earn coveted college degrees. Research shows that mothers like Linda often cite their children as their primary motivation to achieve in school and work.[3] Their kids keep them going, even when they are exhausted, late at night. Yet mothers also understood that the journey to and through higher education is much easier for affluent students. Numerous moms echoed Linda's questions: Do the people who get to make up the rules—politicians, policy makers, and academic leaders—expect *their* children to do everything that they routinely demand of low-income parents in college? Why do they have such a different set of standards for working poor students who are raising children?

"They don't even ask..."

Jocelyn, a twenty-three-year-old Pacific Islander single mom of a preschooler, was astonished that parenthood was a nonissue as she applied to college. "You know, they don't even ask if you have a child," Jocelyn said. "They ask about ethnicity and gender, and about all these other things. But there's no place where you can check 'I am raising a child.'" Whereas student athletes at many colleges and universities may receive free tutoring or early registration because of their extracurricular time commitments, parenting status is typically not recorded, nor does it trigger any institutional support or benefits. A thirty-two-year-old daughter of Mexican immigrants, Adrianna was the first person in her family to go to college. She said that when visiting campuses with a child in tow, she was "out of order" on the campus. The cluster of visiting students might have their parents with them, or friends, but a toddler was an anomaly. Looking back, she says, "There's no way I would have made it if I hadn't had my mother and grandmother. They [administrators and professors] don't expect you to have children."

Like many of the moms we spoke with, Jocelyn described the panic she experienced during the semester when her son became ill with pneumonia and she "dropped a whole letter grade." Employers, school administrators, and faculty—no one, it seemed to Jocelyn, cared about or even recognized that she was a mother. "There is no understanding about what we face," she said. The pile-on of demands from work, school, and a seriously ill child just about ended her college effort. "My scholarship depends on my grades. My [state] childcare depends on my working twenty hours a week."

According to the IWPR, each state has its own tangle of rules and regulations dictating which types of education programs low-income moms are able to pursue and what work requirements they must fulfill in order to receive public benefits, including childcare subsidies.[4] Some states even impose time limits on degree acquisition, despite research that shows parenting students take longer than traditional students to complete degree programs.[5] Jocelyn described getting through a difficult period by holding on to the belief that a college degree is the only way out. "This is how I am going to better our lives," she said. But she reflected sadly that other mothers in her classes couldn't manage the heavy load and dropped out. The majority of parents we interviewed fell into the more than 90 percent of student parents who, despite trying, had not yet completed a degree within six years. Many of the moms we spoke with were on their fourth, fifth, or even sixth try.

Breaking the Cycle of Locking Poor Women Out

Adrianna, the single mother attending college in 2016, had been on an advisory board for low-income parents at her university. She would gather with other mothers to share struggles and strategies. Listening to their stories, she began to develop a critical view about the systemic absence of support for low-income mothers. She thought it reflected a societal attitude that women like herself shouldn't be in college in the first place. In fact, research shows and our conversations across the country confirmed that low-income mothers are often steered away from pursuing degrees and into full-time work or certificate programs, despite the fact that four-year degrees offer the most long-term benefits and economic security.[6] While not a guarantee, on average, obtaining a college degree means increased lifetime earnings and leads to lower rates of unemployment and less need for public assistance. This has an important effect on families most likely to be poor—single-mother families. Calculations by the IWPR show that single mothers who receive an associate's degree on average earn $8,000 a year more than those with only a high school degree—over a lifetime this adds up to $329,500. Single moms who get a bachelor's degree earn $18,500 more each year, relative to a high school diploma, adding up to $610,300 over a lifetime of work.

Importantly, many of the mothers we interviewed pointed out that dollars were only part of the picture. Most of them were the first generation of college students in their working-class and low-income families. They saw themselves as pioneers blazing a path not only for their children but for their siblings, nieces, and nephews. They also pointed out that success getting an associate's degree often led to going for a bachelor's and, for some, then pursuing a graduate degree. This progress would have a dramatic impact on future earnings and quality of work life. But as Katherine Pohlidal, the white director of the Women with Children program at Misericordia University, told us, among most first-generation college students, the world of higher education is a social class mystery.

Knowledge about applying to colleges, applying for financial aid, and—if you manage those initial hurdles—fitting into campus culture is know-how embedded in affluent culture and often absent from the low-income world. The norms and processes surrounding college life were obscure and even frightening to the student parents we met, especially since many of them did not know anyone who had graduated from college.

One young mother from Texas, Lola, told us she felt overwhelmed when she first arrived on campus to learn that in college "you go from classroom to classroom, different buildings, all over the whole campus." She had attended a small rural high school, made it through college, and now, six years later, was entering a graduate program in gerontology. She and several other student parents told us it took time to build confidence and learn how to navigate the culture of complex demands and obscure language. Nobody on a college campus takes the time to define phrases like office hours and academic expectations; students are just expected to understand what is required of them. As Lola put it, "Like, what are 'credit hours' and my 'concentration'; shit, I didn't know what I was concentrating on." But when low-income students did gain this insider knowledge, it could be quickly passed on to their children, younger siblings, and others in their families. Watching an older sibling or aunt overcome obstacles made it seem possible for them. A twenty-five-year-old college student mom in Oregon said, "After I was making it through college, both my sister and brother went too."

Kids Don't Count

Linda and Adrianna and dozens of other mothers in college whom we interviewed pointed out that major financial aid programs largely ignored the cost of children in their aid packages. In fact, the Free Application for Federal Student Aid (FAFSA), the main instrument for assessing student financial need, has pages of questions about parents' assets and potential contribution to college and liabilities that reduce family budgets. For example, the fact that families may have more than one child attending college is treated as a significant strain on their budget and leads to increased financial aid. But there is a single question, only recently added, about whether an applying student is carrying the enormous cost of raising a child while they attend college. In fact, financial aid officers advise that the intention of college aid is to cover the costs of higher education including tuition, housing, required fees, books, labs, and so forth—not to pay for kids' needs.

Don't they get it, Adrianna asked, that all the other costs of college are secondary to knowing your kids are in good care? Childcare is the cornerstone for student parents. None of the women we interviewed who described the time-consuming process of looking for "childcare scholarships" actually got one. Despite the growing demand nationally, campus childcare has declined significantly over the last decade and much of what exists is very expensive. According to the IWPR, campus childcare meets only about 5 percent of the need among students, with more availability among community colleges.[7] On those campuses that do offer on-campus childcare centers, the average waiting list has eighty-two children on it.

The most common advice that mothers received was that they should seek state-funded childcare designed for low-income parents, but the programs vary by state and are extremely difficult to qualify for and maintain. In Oregon, one of the states where we conducted many of the student parent interviews, the state childcare program is called Employment Related Day Care (ERDC). The name immediately announces the program goal. This is not a social mobility program or an investment in human capital, and it is certainly not a program seeking to interrupt intergenerational poverty. It is designed to provide highly regulated childcare subsidies to ensure low-income parents, mostly mothers, remain primarily rooted in the low-wage labor market, even as they go to college. To qualify for this subsidy program, parents must work at least twenty hours per week but keep their income under the set level, be attending college at least half time, maintain a good grade point average, avoid interruptions or withdrawals, and graduate within a set period. Following up on dozens of mothers' stories, we wondered how many parents were actually able to meet and sustain these eligibility requirements through college. As it turns out, less than 1 percent of all families receiving ERDC childcare in 2018 were student parent families. We were reminded of Linda's challenge: *Do they even want us to get through?*

"I had to take one for the team."

Lisa met Kristina in 2017 during her senior year studying child development. A thirty-year-old white woman, Kristina brought her four-year-old daughter, Lila, along. They headed to a local park near Kristina's on-campus housing so Lila could play as they talked. Over the afternoon, Kristina reflected on the obstacles that she faced through three years of college to get to where she was that day. It was her "third try," Kristina said. Born in Idaho, Kristina finished high school and went to a local community college, but "wasn't really ready. Nobody could tell me what to do." But she added that she couldn't recall a single conversation in high school about college planning or what she might be able to do with a degree.

The other issue that demanded her attention was her family. "My mother wasn't well, and I was the oldest. I'd always helped take care of my brothers, and I was really the one raising my baby sister." When Kristina tried college the second time, she was in a management program while also working in fast food and doing a lot of childcare. After a year, she dropped out again. "I started dating and hanging out. I was doing stupid stuff." Looking back, Kristina thinks that she needed more support and guidance and less responsibility for other people's problems. She didn't go into detail about her parents' issues but said that her father became unemployed and her mother became "dysfunctional." Kristina's account of juggling her family's needs while trying to go back to school and create a life for herself reminded us of Alania, who adopted her siblings, and Bella, who was left alone at home with sisters and brothers as her parents chased any job that they could get.

Kristina then mentioned a phrase that her parents used

while she was growing up, that she had to "take one for the team." In her family, this meant she had to come home early from high school and forgo extracurriculars or school activities. When she was juggling jobs and college, it meant that she needed to work her schedule around the needs of her family, particularly her toddler sister. We heard about "taking one for the team" from other women too, as a catchall of gendered sacrifice that, looking back, cost them a lot.

At twenty-six, after much effort, Kristina moved away from her family and entered an undergraduate child development program in Oregon. She focused on early childhood trauma and special needs and hoped to continue on to a graduate degree. Kristina had chosen this university because, at that time, it had a program that offered housing for a few student parent families. So essentially Kristina had "won the lottery!" because she was able to go to college with her six-year-old daughter and infant Lila.

> Lisa: Oh, I missed that. I didn't realize you have two children.
>
> Kristina: Yes, well, I applied to get housing and childcare for two children. They don't know that Tracy is my baby sister, but I raise her, you know. I am her mother, and I wasn't leaving her behind.

Supports Under Fire

Though few and far between, some private and state programs aim at helping parents on public assistance get through college and move out of poverty. Some program outcomes suggest how this population may thrive when supported. The nonprofit Jeremiah Program operates campuses in Minnesota, Texas, North Dakota, Massachusetts, and New York that offer a range of services for student moms including housing, tutoring, career guidance, and early childhood education for their kids. The program has been highly successful, though costly, so the numbers of women and children served remains relatively small. Still, the average annual income of graduates from 2014 to 2019 of the Jeremiah Program is $47,609, whereas the federal poverty guideline for a family of two is $17,420.

Parents as Scholars (PaS) is a state-funded program designed to help low-income student parents who are recipients of welfare benefits to pursue a two- or four-year college degree. Students who participate in PaS receive a range of support services, including transportation, childcare, required books, and supplies that are not covered by financial aid grants. As a rule, PaS does not pay tuition, though individual colleges frequently provide students with financial aid application assistance. However, when students are unable to receive any financial aid, they can get up to $3,500 per academic year from PaS. Students also receive cash benefits equal to TANF cash benefits.

PaS was established in Maine in 1996 and in Oregon in 2008. In Maine, the program continues today and is administered through the state TANF office, serving roughly 700 students. The Maine program has survived several attempts by Republican lawmakers seeking to cut program funding, according to the *Bangor Daily News* in 2014, "to reduce abuse and fraud in Maine's welfare programs." The same article quoted former PaS student parent and now attorney Heidi Hart, who testified in front of the Health and Human Services Committee about the importance of the program: "From my earliest memories, poverty was a familiar state of affairs, and I can still recall the shame that I felt as a child because of my family's financial struggles. . . . I started working full time just two days after my graduation, and I left the welfare rolls for good. . . . As a taxpaying citizen, my lifelong contribution to this state will far outweigh the short-term investment that was made in me through the [PaS] program. The expected course of my daughter's life was also dramatically changed because of the wise decision that Maine made back in 1996 to create this program and provide a lifeline to people like me." A Center for Postsecondary and Economic Success (C-PES, part of the Center for Law and Social Policy) analysis of a 2001 cohort of PaS students showed they earned significantly more than mothers who had not gone to college.

The PaS program in Oregon, however, was not successful in warding off attempts to cut program funding. In fact, it stopped accepting new parents after only three years. We researched the abrupt end to the state program in 2017. With some effort, we obtained the "PaS Outcome" report, a two-page document that was the basis for evaluating the program as a failure. Over the life of the program, fewer than six hundred families had been accepted and started school. While there was no narrative explaining the numbers, the brief report recorded that 117 parents had been discontinued (with no information on cause for termination); 163 were no longer on public assistance, a requirement for continued eligibility; and 133 had experienced interruptions or withdrawals in their college progress and so were no longer eligible. Ten percent or 59 parents had graduated from college. These raw numbers were hard to interpret, but in meetings with state program administrators, a view was expressed that the moms were taking too long to get through college and there was a suspicion that they were using the program to get childcare and to avoid low-wage jobs. In other words, there was a sense they were gaming the system.

We thought about all the obstacles moms had described to us: children's illness, extended family demands, coursework that required extra time for which they had no childcare, housing disruptions, moments of despair, and constant meetings to be "reevaluated" for eligibility to continue to receive help. It seemed premature, after three years, to judge them as failures. Sonya, a first-generation African American student in 2017, described the difficult path she and other poor mothers face trying to leave poverty jobs behind. Sonya didn't suggest that there was any particular conspiracy to lock them out. But she pointed out that, in practice, poor mothers—who are often single parents, disproportionately women of color, and who come from low-income and working-class families—are constantly judged, regulated, and denied. Sonya summed it up by saying, "Maybe they're just keeping us in our place," a place that doesn't include a college degree and a good job.

A Different Route to Better Jobs

Not everyone wants to go to college—but that doesn't mean they want to stay stuck in dead-end jobs. In 2019 into 2020, we interviewed women who were in apprenticeship or pre-apprenticeship programs for building trades jobs. Pre-apprenticeship programs prepare people, mostly women, who want to apply for apprenticeships in the building trades. These women had their sights set on becoming electricians, carpenters, plumbers, pipefitters, and drywall installers. A journeyman carpenter or electrician starts at an annual income of around $54,000 and gradually earns more, easily double the income of most of the mothers we had interviewed over the years.

Ella was one of the women we met who was focused on getting into "the trades." A single mom of three children, in 2021 Ella said that "after COVID, I will be able to do work [as an electrician] that more than doubles what I made working two jobs. I just cannot wait, I'm telling you right now. Like the benefits. My kids need dental. I'm looking forward to working one job with benefits, and I am not even worried because, well . . . honestly, I am very nervous because I am a girl and Hispanic. You know, there's gonna be people that are not gonna be happy. *I really don't care. I'm going to get my stuff done.* It's gonna change for me and my kids."

Ella, like most women we met in building trades programs, raised the issue of being "a girl" in a sea of majority white men. Most women seemed to include in their decision-making what they knew would be a certain level of stereotyping and possibly harassment, which they rationalized they could handle in exchange for what these jobs could get them. Alice, a white mother in her midtwenties, said that having "been in the armed forces, I knew what to expect. I knew to just pretend you don't hear some stuff. And you know who's okay and who you don't want to be alone with" at work. For women of color, sexist jokes and the "getting into your space" behavior of some men might be infused with racism too, often packaged as friendly banter. Nicola, a Black woman in her forties, said that she seethed when white men made "playful" remarks that "are racist but are supposed to be funny." She added that even more common was sexist talk from both white and Black male co-workers, references to her body, her weight, and how she looks on the job. But reacting with anger takes more away than it offers a woman on those work sites. Being seen as over-sensitive is understood by tradeswomen as self-destructive, or, as Alice put it, "If you act like a girl, you won't be part of the team. I know what that means from serving [in the military]." Echoing working poor mothers in college, these women talked about holding on to the big-picture goal: jobs that pay a living wage.

Some of what these women described could be considered actionable grounds to make a legal complaint about sexual harassment, bullying, or racial discrimination. As one electrician, an organizer for her union, put it, "It's so fucked up what we still have to put up with . . . they [male leadership] treat it like it's a joke." Far more important to these working moms was making the climb through a GED, pre-apprenticeship, and then apprenticeship program to get the prize of a sustainable income. Passing all the tests and evaluations was just a start. If you got through, then you had to be considered a good and reliable worker, a desirable member of a work-site team dominated by men. And the person who decided who was reliable, a team player, a good worker, was almost always a man.

This gender disparity is reflected in national numbers; in 2018, just 3.4 percent of workers in the construction trades were women.[8] In the state of Oregon, where we met most women in the trades, the Oregon Tradeswomen has been leading statewide efforts to bring women, particularly BIPOC women, into these well-paid union jobs. They have been working to increase women's numbers for three decades, and in 2021, 8 percent of the trade workforce in Oregon was female, more than twice the national average. Still, this is a tiny percentage of a job sector that could economically transform working poor families—particularly single-mother families. It is uphill work. Among the women we met, the tales of being marginalized, harassed, and sometimes abused tell how much of this BIPOC people and women still face. But these moms' stories tell us more. They tell what mothers in particular must silently endure to climb their way into sustainable jobs.

Alice's advice was to ignore bigoted comments, even "creepy" behavior, as the price a woman had to pay to get a living wage. We had heard similar advice three years earlier from Brianna, a twenty-five-year-old white mom in college. Brianna had made it through the Marines as "part of the 7 percent of new Marines that were women." In one of our conversations, Brianna made it clear that she was not going to go into any detail about her experiences while in boot camp. She just said, "Everything you hear about what they put girls through, it's all true." The prize for three years in the Marines was military benefits that no other pathway would have provided. She was able to get college tuition, housing assistance, childcare, health insurance, and more. Brianna, who came from a tiny rural town in Texas, said, "All the girls I met were there [boot camp] for the same reason. It was the only way we could get ahead."

Alice, Nicola, and Brianna took similar approaches to make it through. Ignore the noise, keep a low profile, don't make a big deal out of sexist and racist language and being harassed by bullies as long as it doesn't get *too bad*. But, we wondered, what is too bad for these young women who keep children's survival at the center of everything? Desperate to get ahead, they likely experienced some of the worst of #MeToo moments but stayed silent. Across the board, women who had been in the military, in college, and in apprenticeship programs advised, above all, keeping your eye on a future free from poverty jobs. The challenge was just holding on and getting there when you are also raising children, particularly if you are doing it alone. Alice said, "Try not to tell anyone you're a single mother," because right away, "you are going to the back of the line" for jobs.

Making It Up the Ladder

In early 2020, Lisa talked with Aurora about her attempt to pursue an apprenticeship to "ease into this world of construction." Aurora said the pre-apprenticeship was a "great program because you know, mostly women, we don't know about construction. I stumbled upon it when I was researching just how to . . . get started in the trade as a woman and I found it. I'm so glad I did." Aurora had long recognized that the low-wage jobs she had been working would never lead to anything but more of the same. They offered no ladder to a better life. "So it's a program that's intended to help women enter the trade, as well as people that might have disabilities, veterans, young people that may need extra help getting into the trade."

She described the interview process and her excitement to be accepted into a group of sixteen with only two men. "It was great. It was a ten-week course that we would go into the training center every day, and they have labs. They taught us basic, how to use hand tools, how to read a tape measure, things that maybe women were never even shown. And so, it really helped [me] ease into this world of construction, and it's a totally different world from the other jobs I'd had. You showed up every day and did what you were supposed to do, then you took the aptitude test. Now after that, you were accepted into the apprenticeship [from the pre-apprenticeship program into apprenticeships in different trades] and from there, you're hired on with the company and you go to work right away."

Aurora's description was very positive. Being in a class of women, she explained, who could admit they were new to hammers and power drills, gave her the confidence to keep going. But when she turned to the inevitable collision course with mothers' care work, her tone turned from enthusiasm to frustration about the difficulty of making the hours work without family to step in "if you don't have resources as backup." Aurora explained, "I found myself in a situation where the childcare I had wasn't open on certain holidays, so it left me in a position where I had to figure it out, and I actually had to tell them, 'Okay, this is the situation.' It got to the point where I called the [pre-apprentice training program staff] crying. I mean I was in tears. And there's just amazing people at the training center. Thankfully, I talked to somebody over there. And I said, 'I can't do it anymore. I can't do it.' I only see my kid for an hour a day. I don't know how to balance this out. I am a single parent. He doesn't have anybody else."

That was it. Aurora left the program and moved out of state, back to "where I knew that there would be family members that would be able to help with him. I didn't want to leave. But I was running out of any childcare help. So knowing that, I made the choice that I felt was best for my son . . . even if maybe not for me," she said. Aurora realized she had to give up her chance because, even though in the end her family would be better off, children's lives cannot be put aside for a couple of years. Their everyday needs and vulnerabilities always come first. Yet the way this is framed in public narratives is with words like "dropouts," "no-shows," or, in fancier terms, women who haven't developed executive function or lack autonomy or haven't gained "agency." As a union advocate said, "It's easy to look at them like they haven't made the grade, like they've failed. But no one knows what they have to deal with, every day."

Single Moms Need Support

Over the years, we heard countless mothers describe how the help and support of their own mothers or other family members was essential to their efforts to move ahead in the trades. In November of 2020, Pamela, a white single mom with two children living in Washington, recognized family help was the only way she was able to try to break into the construction field. "I didn't have a choice. If you're a single mom you're juggling this all on your own. If my mom hadn't been able to help out, I'd have gone back in the hole, back to welfare."

Pamela still juggled care for her two kids, ages two and seven, while trying to make a good impression in this male-dominated world. "It was a struggle, finding care that opened early enough for me to be able to get to where I needed to be on time. You know, that put a damper on how well I performed, of course, and my employer, you know—some employers are understanding, but it gets old pretty fast. It's not really that important to them. Like the guys, and it's really all guys, they have someone at home who does all of that. You know, if you have childcare near the job or your family, whatever . . . but if not, it's not workable. But you know, potentially if my job is close to the childcare, it could be right."

When Pamela was pregnant with her second child, she had fallen off a ladder while on the job. "It wasn't high up; still, it was an issue." After that, she felt as though she was being excluded. "I was okay, fine, but they stopped sending me off to jobs. They sent out this kid I know to fill in . . . he didn't have kids or pregnancy they'd have to deal with." Pamela understood concern about a pregnant woman being injured on the job and the worries about liability. But she also thought there could be ways to keep her working productively without risk. To them, "it just wasn't worth the hassle."

Alice, who had served in the military before joining the building trades, also talked about this culture created by men at the top. The heads of the labor unions and some of the construction company leaders will say they "want diversity . . . or, you know, they're all in on equity." But equity is more than words. According to Alice, if they, the unions and employers, want "women to move ahead," they have to "make childcare or make schedules that work for taking care of kids." She pointed out too that "big shots" in the construction business and labor unions have the money and know-how to create childcare space. Build a daycare center on-site and pay childcare workers well, and you would have women line up to work for you. Deja, an African American union organizer, said, "If we had Black women in leadership, you *know* that issues like childcare and being a single mother and health, they'd all be in the front. That's our lives," but, "you know how it goes, white men who run the unions and the companies and really wealthy white women too, they don't like to let go of the power."

Family Keeps You Going

Pamela faced a hard choice. She had to "send my son" to another city to be cared for by his paternal grandmother. "I know he's okay, but he wants to come home." She said, "I don't want a pity party," but the people who are running the jobs "need to *get* the daily struggles" moms face. She said, "I am sad all the time with my son away. Sad, you know. I am frustrated. I did everything I could do to get where I am, and I can't provide for them."

So for a while, Pamela's mom stepped in. She would arrive at 6:00 a.m. so Pamela could leave for work and arrive by 6:30 a.m. Her mom would feed her grandchildren breakfast, then drop them off at two separate places, school and childcare. On a regular schedule, Pamela would get off work in time to pick them up. But being the person on the work site not willing to take additional hours reflects badly on you. She didn't want to be the one person walking off the job when all the others stayed, so many days Pamela would have to call her mother to do pickup too and bring them home to wait for her. She knew that it was becoming a lot to ask of her mom. But without her she would have to give up.

The need for ad hoc childcare when they were running late or asked to work extra hours kept many of the moms relying on family members who were more flexible than daycare centers. In chapter 2, Ella, a thirty-three-year-old Mexican mom of three, told us about running between her two jobs at Pizza Hut and a call center. Right away, she wanted to discuss what had pushed her to leave the low-wage labor market and pursue becoming an apprentice electrician. She opened with, "I am a single mom, you know." This was a self-designation that we heard frequently. It is a particular mother identity indicating a life that, even among struggling low-income mothers, is understood to be a whole other level of hard. You have less than half the money and you manage the kids alone. One in four children in the United States lives in a home with a single parent. The poverty rate for single-parent families is roughly five times greater than the rate for families headed by married parents. Both parenting alone and struggling to make ends meet financially add significantly to family stress, according to the American Psychological Association.[9]

Ella went on, "My parents would help me by keeping my middle daughter and picking my son up from school. I would get off, you know, from my first job and go home to be with them for a little bit and then run back to my other job." Ella worked weekends too. "I couldn't keep up with it for, like, too long. What happened actually was that the company [the call center] got sold. They fired all the people that were not permanent. So, I got laid off that job. By then . . . I was really, really, really tired."

That's when Ella jumped at the opportunity to do a pre-apprentice program, hoping to become an electrician. Describing this chance and how she built up her confidence to apply, Ella mentioned Jackie Whitt, who coordinates a pre-apprenticeship program. But as we listened to Ella and several other women seeking a trade, it became clear that Jackie was more than her position indicates. She "knows how hard it is," and she "doesn't give up on you." Talking with Jackie, her commitment is clear. But so is her understanding that women—particularly single moms, women of color, and women who have lived with abuse—are the most likely to be shut out of any opportunity for advancement. Jackie was one of several advocates we met who described their realization that advocacy must turn into something stronger.

"You have to do more than talk."

Time and again, all over the country, we heard stories about people like Jackie, who go way beyond conventional roles to provide services or to advocate for poor mothers and children. They popped up in the bios of dozens of women trying to find childcare or get through college or make it into trade jobs, and sometimes the help they provided was said to be lifesaving. We heard about Katherine in Pennsylvania and Autumn in Massachusetts, who have designed their own job descriptions determined to help mothers get through college. They used all the resources available and then they made some up. We heard about Dee, a homecare worker who never sits still because she is always standing up for and with other homecare workers, many BIPOC mothers and grandmothers who earn poverty wages. And Trudy, who advises poor parents how to get subsidized childcare and finds ways around state rules designed to minimize aid to struggling families; she's became a workaround artist. When their names came up, often we would hear, "If she hadn't been there all the time telling me that I would make it" and "Hard as it was, there's no way I'd have made it through if she hadn't been there." They were advocates but went far beyond that soft title. They would go to bat hard and, when necessary, subvert the many rules that drag mothers down. They designed underground tactics, quietly putting the rights and well-being of poor women and children before all else.

These advocates are largely invisible in mainstream culture, but mothers described their profound impact in helping them keep on going. Women said that personal determination, availability of family to help out, luck, and sometimes a rare, flexible program were critical factors that gave them a chance. But to have someone on your side who gets what you face and is willing to really jump in, maybe go over the line—this was irreplaceable in pushing back against a mountain of inequities.

When we shared some of these women's comments with the advocates, they tended to minimize their role and circle back to the strength and solidarity of working poor mothers. Katherine Pohlidal from Misericordia University put it like this: women "worked with one another and actually helped each other," which challenges "the assumption they're not going to get along. They are so used to fighting for every little thing. But it was the opposite. They were finding the connectivity, you know, Black women and white women. They build kinship. They know [what] the other moms are facing. We help, of course, but they build a group and create that group self-esteem, a group identity which is positive and empowered. There's conflict too of course. But give these moms a chance, and they rebuild."

8

Calling Us Up

During the height of COVID, lawn signs and banners thanked essential workers, like the grocery store clerks and cleaning staff who did the "deep cleans." We relied on them so we could send our kids back into schools or to childcare centers while we worked virtually. We depended on them to stock shelves and deliver prepared food and tend our elderly kin in residential facilities. But where are these essential workers now?

Danielle faced near-constant anxiety working as a grocery cashier through the pandemic. At first, her employers seemed to acknowledge her risk. For three months in 2020, she received hazard pay, which amounted to an extra two and then one dollar per hour. But then, even though the hazards remained, the extra pay stopped. "I'm going to work risking my life every day. We don't get hazard pay anymore. And there's been no stimulus package or stimulus bill put into place that even gives any type of retroactive hazard pay to frontline workers or anything," she said.

The low-income moms we've listened to for years started capturing headlines in 2020, their faces plastered across magazines and newspapers. Stars of the pandemic, working moms reported about life stuck at home with kids, worried about paying bills; they opened up for the cameras about bone-deep exhaustion coming home from overnight shifts to fill cereal

bowls and monitor Zoom school. Citizen-reporter moms standing in laundry and living rooms streamed video straight from their iPhones onto CNN. And the public reacted. While the spotlight always eventually strayed to higher-income people's pandemic woes, the extreme hardships experienced by low-wage mothers were suddenly spotlighted too. The pandemic unmasked profound inequities that riddle U.S. society.

Against all of this exposure, we found ourselves asking: Will these millions of women and their children be forgotten as the post-pandemic recovery unfolds? Does getting back to normal mean reasserting wage poverty, cutting eviction protection, throwing low-income kids back into childcare chaos? We reached out to a diverse group of experts, community leaders, and advocates to hear their thoughts about these questions and the way forward.

Who Gets Left Out?

The emergency paid leave provision of the Families First Coronavirus Response Act (FFCRA) was intended to keep essential employees from being penalized when they put their children and families first after daycare centers and schools closed. But there were exemptions, for both businesses employing fewer than 50 people and those employing more than 500 people. In effect, these exemptions denied many essential workers any childcare relief. The *Washington Post* reported that the way the law was written exempted from job protections some 7.4 million workers in very large companies and another 2.4 million workers in small companies: "Only 12 percent of workers in essential industries work for companies that will be guaranteed coverage by the bill. The problem is particularly acute for general merchandise companies, such as Target and Walmart."[1] These labor protection exceptions—if the business is small or very large or carved out in some other way—riddle our labor laws.

At the end of 2020, the Brookings Institution reported that the "pandemic has generated record profits for America's biggest companies, as well as immense wealth for their founders and largest shareholders—but next to nothing for workers."[2] They go on to say that while raking in billions during the pandemic, companies "shared little of that windfall with their frontline workers, who risk their lives each day for wages that are often so low they can't support a family."[3] Reflecting this, Danielle recalled watching the price of groceries going up in her store during the shutdown. "After I pay bills and get food, it's like I'm broke. I'm already waiting for the next paycheck. It's like the grocery store chains are actually taking advantage of the pandemic too, because they were able to raise food prices. And what is the average person going to say, 'Well, oh, no, I can't buy food.' Because everyone is home, so you kind of have no choice," she said.

Unions representing services, food, care, and grocery workers were keeping a critical eye on what recovery means to low-wage workers and their families. Kroger, the biggest supermarket chain in the United States, has seen profits soar over the pandemic years. The company rewarded its CEO with a salary bump raising his annual income to over $20 million. But a survey of more than 10,000 frontline Kroger workers, commissioned by the United Food and Commercial Workers Union, revealed that 75 percent of them experience food insecurity and 14 percent have experienced homelessness. During the pandemic, Kroger had passed out gift cards as "appreciation pay" and "heroes bonuses." Yet, as the report goes on to say, many workers are running out of food before the end of the month, skipping meals, and going hungry to make sure their children eat. They spend their days handling food that brings in billions to Kruger shareholders and top management while being paid so little they go hungry.[4]

Labor leaders are shining a light on who gets left out when employers use these divisive tactics. They call out pitting seasoned workers against new hires and—since workers of color are often newer hires—pitting white and BIPOC workers against each other. Cassie Geremaia, a union organizer for the Service Employees International Union (SEIU) in Colorado, pushed such divisiveness aside. "Here's the truth: we've always been essential. When we look back at how we beat this pandemic, we'll know that it wasn't corporate CEOs or billionaires that came through and saved us. It was health care workers, janitors, public employees, and other workers who risk our lives for others," she said.

In 2020, these workers were acknowledged and celebrated. But what about now? Sade Moonsammy, who is an African American woman and deputy director of the working women's rights organization Family Values at Work, pointed out, "This pandemic has made abundantly clear that what was considered 'normal' wasn't working for most families—certainly not for women of color." She and other activists with whom we spoke raised hard questions, directed particularly to those of us who identify as pro "diversity, equity, and inclusion," or as anti-racists and feminists, even as liberals and Democrats.

They call us up to do more. To build solidarity and to ensure the recovery is not built on the backs of working poor people.

Reaching Across Class Lines

There have been some notable cross-race and class stands in recent years. For a few exciting days in 2019, before a pandemic swept through the country, some women were building cross-class solidarity in the most ordinary place imaginable. It started in grocery store aisles across the Northeast, where moms across income brackets shop to feed their families. In the pre-pandemic months, the United Food and Commercial Workers International Union at Stop & Shop stores won their biggest labor victory to date, following an eleven-day strike across New England. The labor union organized the action, but it was ordinary people, mostly moms, standing on both sides of the grocery counters that brought about victory.

"We were just trying to maintain what we had, and of course, get a general wage increase, but they were trying to take away pensions and no longer cover spouses on health and welfare," said Jessica Petronella, a local union representative in Connecticut. Stop & Shop, like many other major corporations, is trying to take away benefits from low-wage workers. It is looking for a way to increase corporate profit by reducing spending on thousands of employees. These employees are the people who, months later, would be called our essential workers.

All of the affluent moms we spoke with in the New England area recalled this moment of labor conflict. Some talked about feeling connected to the cashiers who made up a racially diverse workforce in stores located in majority white areas. Moms on both sides of the counter might ask about each other's kids whom they'd been hearing about over the years. They might share moments of pride and times of worry, a common ground of motherhood. So when these working women walked off the job, and many were visible on the picket lines along with their children, some affluent moms drove into the parking lot, saw them, and then turned around. One mom said she brought back coffee and donuts for the picketers. Others said they encouraged friends to stop shopping there. Gradually, the parking lots of Stop & Shops across New England emptied in solidarity. "The customer support was key. I don't think any of us thought we would get the customer support that we did . . . I mean, *we really had virtually nobody crossing the picket line*," said Petronella.

Shopping elsewhere was an inconvenience to these consumers, a small one: it cost them time to turn around and adjust to unfamiliar food shopping, even temporarily. It meant changing a routine that is hardwired for most food shoppers. But the idea of crossing a picket line of working parents who earn such low wages shifted something. It made sense to disrupt a routine that had become complicit with mistreating hardworking moms and dads. And pretty quickly, participating in disruption became something of value for the suburban, higher-income women who acted on it. The workers took a risk standing up for themselves and, in some cases, stopping paychecks their families vitally needed; recognizing this public stand, consumers chose to stand with them. And the union— and the working poor people it represented—won.

In another institutional setting—a university—a similar

cross-class effort took shape. Eve Weinbaum, a union leader and a white professor at the University of Massachusetts, pointed out how motherhood can be a catalyst for uniting women across class and race. Weinbaum says that for years there has been "a lot of pressure on women faculty not to take parental leave, not to talk about their kids, or put up family pictures in their office." She added, "It's pretty clear there is still discrimination against women who have kids." Pushing back, Weinbaum promotes making motherhood and family more visible at work. "It helps everyone for you to say, 'I had a baby and I am going up for tenure.'" While it is important to challenge systematic discrimination against women faculty, even more numerous on campuses everywhere are the nonsalaried, lower-income employees, often without a union to back them. And they are far more vulnerable.

At Eve's university, for example, aside from other privileges like sabbaticals and research leave time, faculty could qualify for a semester of paid parental leave. Professional staff could apply for up to six months through a leave bank. But mirroring corporate patterns of inequality, low-wage classified staff only qualified for ten days. Eve said that when the faculty learned of the unfair treatment of the lowest-earning workers, many were outraged. "Gaining widespread support for a campaign to treat all parents and kids equally was not easy," she said. But support for their campaign took off after they held a panel of faculty and staff talking about their experiences. "Most people were supportive once they knew what was going on." And the coalition was effective, winning an expansion of leave benefits for classified workers at the university. Yet alongside teaching, tending to their own families, publishing in their fields, and meeting all the academic standards of success, worrying about the lives of other workers on campus has too often been an afterthought for faculty. As Weinbaum explains, that can change. As other activists told us, if we are serious about equity it *must* change.

Care Can Unite Us

One issue that brings diverse working families together is an overwhelming need for care labor. Irina, a homecare worker in the Northwest, put it this way. The need for care is "where we all will be at some point. Needing some help and maybe you don't have family that can drop everything. You will need us. And we need you. We need decent pay for all we do." Researchers predict the aging of the baby boom generation could result in as much as a 75 percent increase in the number of elderly, for example, needing care. "There is such a shortage of home-care workers and increasing demand for them. People don't want to wind up in nursing homes. This is a great opportunity to bring multiple constituencies together who all have a stake in this fight because they don't want their mom to end up in a nursing home or they don't want to end up in one," said Julie Solow, an organizer for Hand in Hand in New York. Hand in Hand is a national network of domestic employers who work "hand in hand" with their domestic workers to fight for better pay, policies, and working conditions. For care workers like Irina, it makes sense that the family members of those receiving care would stand up for home health aides whose average hourly wage is between $12 and $14. They should be outraged that women working in nursing homes, for example, are routinely paid so little to handle the most intimate end of life care.

Service Employees International Union organizers have long recognized the connection between people who give and people who get care, and they work to make this connection visible. In Boston, in 2012, organizers bused dozens of home-care workers and care consumers to speak to Massachusetts policy makers. We walked with them that day, entering the statehouse where both workers and consumers took the podium together. Disabled professionals, elders, and their relatives described what would happen if they did not get the help that homecare workers provide. Then care workers spoke of long relationships with their clients, their commitment and attachment, essential to good care. But they also talked about low wages, precarious work schedules, and no job benefits. One wheelchair-bound African American professional told the large audience, "I would need welfare if not for her," referring to the Caribbean homecare worker standing next to him. Instead he was making a decent income and contributing to the state economy. So he asked the crowd, "Why doesn't she deserve a living wage too?"

Our conversations with domestic workers, homecare workers, and nursing home aides confirm the bond often formed between caregivers and their clients. "A lot of people come to advocate for their care workers because they have grown really intimate relationships with them. These people have become a part of their family," said Solow, who organizes in New York's Hudson Valley. At the same time, we also saw how these bonds and family connections could be used to exploit people who are already underpaid. Laura, one of the affluent Connecticut moms we met in chapter 4, recognized the relationships with her children's nannies over the years as deeply significant in the life of her family. "These women are caring for your children, on a daily basis, and in some cases living in your home, so they really do become like an extension of your family."

Laura came to believe that she had a deep responsibility to the women who were helping her raise a family. She helped pay for school, legal advice, and funded loans to different nannies who worked for her. She represented a nanny's family member in court because they couldn't afford to hire an attorney. And yet, she recognized the limitations of even her redesign of the employee-employer relationship. In college, Laura read the book *Between Women: Domestics and Their Employers* by Judith Rollins. "It makes me think about those things around the margins," she said, "like giving paid time off or overtime or holiday pay. The idea that you are living-in so maybe you are supposed to be off, but are at home, so what does that mean if the family wants to go out?" Laura acknowledged that other affluent moms she knows, even some who would call themselves liberal or feminist, don't seem to apply the same ethics when it comes to nannies and others working in their homes. Affluent white culture teaches that we do not have to apply an equity lens to our daily lives; that's a private matter.

The pandemic highlighted this distinction among the well-off. For some, the pandemic disrupted a sacrosanct capitalist credo: always pay as little as you can and never pay for anything you don't get. Suddenly—at least to some people—that seemed wrong. We heard from women who paid domestics and childcare providers during the shutdown even though they were not receiving the services. Others did not. "So many of the moms I know in town just didn't pay their cleaning ladies, like, didn't even think of it because they weren't coming during the pandemic. I mean, I paid my cleaning lady, because how else is she supposed to live?" said Harriet, a white affluent Connecticut mom.

Practices of hyper-exploitation were widely publicized during the pandemic. Childcare workers and home health aides reported being forced to leave their own families and "bubble up" and "live-in" with their employers because of concerns about cross-contamination. In fact, one accounting consultant advised that requiring "help" to live in would "reduce their children's exposure to people outside their homes."[5] The consulting company pointed out that a family can choose to deduct room and board from the live-in wages so long as they meet a minimum standard. It would be safer in a pandemic— and maybe always preferable for affluent households. So working moms like Serena, whom we met in chapter 3, faced the untenable choice of the superexploited: lose all your income, or leave your family to provide care and ensure the safety of your nervous, wealthy clients.

Hand in Hand pointed out that whatever hits higher-income families were taking, nannies, house cleaners, and home-care and eldercare workers were being hurt much more. They called for a commitment from employers that anyone who *could* continue paying their workers should. It was Hand in Hand's Employer Pledge. "We urge individuals and families who employ nannies, house cleaners, and home attendants to protect the rights and livelihood of this workforce by pledging to pay workers even if they are not currently working in your home. As not everyone is able to or will pay domestic workers who are home sick or sheltering in place, consider paying extra if you can." But beyond these private choices, do we have a responsibility to make this a public discussion? Should those of us who identify as pro-equity, anti-racist, and pro-women take this on? A wide range of people told us that's exactly who should.

Breaking Ranks

Josephine Kalipeni, director of Family Values at Work, acknowledged that talking about where we stand makes for some very uncomfortable conversations. Asking affluent, largely white liberals if they would sign a pledge and commit to paying more than they have to breaks class rules. Josephine, a Black African/Malawian, considers it a kind of risk analysis unfamiliar to most white, privileged people. "As a Black woman, I am always facing a risk analysis, all the time." But she and others told us these should be everyone's stakes now. "If there is no cost to you, then you are not stepping up. It's great to be generous and write checks. But a lot more needs to be done." The stakes are high, and that cost should carried by people who have a lot.

Andrea Paluso, the white director of Family Forward in Oregon, agrees with Josie and suggested another angle on cost: "I have to show up for a struggle that isn't about me." This contrasts sharply with the dominant affluent culture, rooted in self-promotion. Particularly, as a white progressive woman, Andrea believes that if you are serious about equity, you are challenged to commit to a struggle that, if won, may mean you give up the front-row seat. "White [people] have to be committed to making space for more inclusive frameworks and also to stepping back so other people can lead in those spaces." Or, as Josephine put it, people with privilege have to ask themselves, "What am I willing to give up?"

Affluent mom Sabrina volunteers for a local nonprofit charged with raising funds and awareness for issues affecting women and girls. She routinely solicits donations and volunteer hours from her peer suburban moms. "These are liberal, educated people, but for some of them it's just easier not to see the poverty among these women—it's easier to just not go there, so they will write a check. It makes them very uncomfortable to see how people are living—right in their backyard basically." Fairfield County, Connecticut, where Sabrina lives, includes the New York City suburbs of Fairfield, Greenwich, Westport, New Canaan, and Darien. Right next door is the run-down city of Bridgeport, with abandoned factories, broken windows, and poverty rates over 20 percent. This pairing within the same county results in some of the worst inequality and biggest wealth gap in the nation.[6]

"You've got a lot of wealthy people, housewives really, who are raising kids in the area while their husbands commute into the city. And many of them are progressive," said Sabrina. Soon after moving to Fairfield, she volunteered to deliver coats to a home in Bridgeport. "I'll never forget walking by these people in the hallway, and the house is literally falling down, and there are mothers with their kids sitting there and the conditions were so awful . . . just knowing it is so close to where we live. I got back into my BMW to drive home to my 4,600-square-foot home—and it literally made me sick. I walked past my own kids, went straight into the bathroom, and threw up." Sabrina thinks this is why some of the moms would rather donate than do anything in person. "It makes them feel guilty, and they want to protect their kids. They don't want them to see it."

Donating instead of volunteering, while still important, may help avoid a true reckoning. Cynthia, a retired white professional on the East Coast, agreed that affluent people find it easy to avoid the real deal. She described first getting involved with an economic mobility program for single mothers. "In the beginning, you hear about the program and think that the women get a lot of free support. Education, housing, and help finding childcare, so, like, they're all set. But, you know, as you get more involved in the program, you find out that that's not the case at all. . . . There are costs of going to work that are huge for them. It seems like a small thing, but I remember them talking at one meeting about women with no dental insurance and no money. They had pain . . . dental problems with a tooth. And too, you know, you don't want to go to a job interview or to classes without some of your teeth. Affluent women don't think about that, they just get their teeth fixed. *I didn't think about it, but I do now.*"

"I think it is the personal that makes us step up."

Lydia, a young white lawyer and mother living in Washington, has worked for immigrant legal rights for years. She told us, "I think it has to get personal for a lot of [middle-class] people. You start to see things differently, like through the eyes of a mother who can't make ends meet. I asked myself, 'What would I do if that was me?' That's personal and you start saying, 'I have to do more.'" She, Laura, and other affluent women told us that, for them, it took getting face-to-face to break through stereotypes they did not realize they held. In their view, "it's the personal" that pushed them from passive support—allies at a distance—to join up. This could mean doing more than boycotting a store, or signing a referendum, or writing a check, or simply voting your values. Passive support is not enough right now, we heard, and you may have to step outside the class or race safety zone. We are called up to do more.

Making it personal is exactly what Jackie Whitt, a multiracial Cherokee citizen woman who coordinates wraparound support for moms trying to move into well-paid union jobs, says needs to happen. But she thinks higher-income people, even those who care, avoid the "personal struggles of others" that are close to home. Talking in the fall of 2021, she mused, "I wonder, instead of families hosting foreign exchange students, why not host a mom and her child for a year, so she can get through a year of college or whatever, without having to worry about housing? Or maybe 'host' an underprivileged child for a year, in a good daycare program, so her mom can get into a better job? Or maybe help out an underserved teen with sports, music, or school clothing for the year, just sponsoring a local child." Jackie continued, "Why do so many equity-minded people avoid the local low-income mom and her child in favor of people far away? Maybe one day I'll quit my job and start a program myself. Maybe I can start a movement!"

While in Pennsylvania in 2020, Lisa talked with a white professional woman, Katrina, who identified as deeply committed to social justice work. Katrina, who has a high-income spouse, was challenging herself—examining her class location in a profoundly unequal society and how that affects the choices that she makes. Katrina led the launching of a wonderful local and mixed-income mothers' group. They connect frequently and share issues, concerns, and advice, but they also physically step in to provide concrete help to one another. Katrina noticed that engagement has made a big impression on some of the higher-income members who had no idea what families living a few miles away were facing.

We asked Katrina, "Do you think this would make them join a campaign for a living wage?"

"This has been on my mind so much, okay," she reflected. "I don't know, and I'm embarrassed to say that, but I don't know. Because I think that to do that, it would come at a cost for them. I think some would. But I don't know. I think others would *want* to and I think that they would say that, that they'd *want to*, but at the end of the day, if it came to really a sacrifice for them . . . closing the gap between, like, between the service worker and that [wealthy] family, I don't know that they would. That's the way I feel. And then it makes me rethink all my friendships and social circle."

Katrina's reflections sounded like the comments that other equity activists made. Sade summed it up in sharp terms. "You may have to lose some people in your life." Evictions are spreading, child poverty is increasing, and wages are rising only slightly, not enough to keep moms and children out of poverty. Taking on hard conversations and even breaking some ties seem like small costs. A decade ago, Reeve, a Black labor organizer, told Lisa that she wanted to call up other women. She talked about hoping the day would come when moms would stand up for other moms, Black, white, and Latinx, middle class and poor. She hoped everyone else who values what moms do would feel compelled to join in. That hope ran through many of our interviews and local community conversations.

Nancy, an affluent white woman from Pennsylvania, spoke of learning from her daughter who was involved in a program that, as Nancy put it, was for "underprivileged children": "My daughter is involved in helping them get into college. She told me about one time a new, a teenage mother she was helping . . . she just had a new baby, and she . . . qualified to get free formula from I think it was the WIC program. And my daughter had called her back, to see if she went to get her free formula, and she didn't. And I said, 'How can that happen? Why wouldn't she go if she could get free formula?' And my daughter said, 'Mom, she had a newborn baby and no one to help, so she'd have to drag this new baby in the freezing cold, she had to go in three buses to go get some formula.' My first reaction was to blame *her*. But you have to ask, what would I do in that situation?"

When professional and affluent moms detailed their struggles, they often added a postscript: "I can't imagine how hard it is for low-income or single moms." This might be said with a shudder and a quick turning away. But we suggest this is the moment to stop and imagine exactly what it is like for millions of mothers and fathers whose labor we rely on all the time. Ellen Bravo, a white leader of economic justice campaigns for women for decades, thinks we should make a point of asking ourselves similar questions in our equity and social justice work. "When we are fighting for better policies for ourselves, at work, are we demanding that same policy for every level of the organization? This should be our starting point," she said.

We challenge readers to work at developing this awareness, asking questions as a first step toward advocacy. When we hear about a college scholarship, ask whether it would cover a single mom who needs childcare as well as tuition. Find out whether the paid family leave at your workplace covers the lowest-waged employee. Ask whether those workers have access to paid sick days—as much as you have. When new childcare policies are proposed, ask whether they consider the needs of working poor mothers and childcare workers. Make sure any campaign for higher wages, paid time off, or other family supports—the ones we know are essential for our families—will reach her family.

Consider if the post-pandemic "recovery" actually treats as essential the needs of the essential workers: the low-wage parents, BIPOC workers, immigrant families, single mothers and their children. Now that we have seen the low-income moms working overnight in warehouses to assemble our packages, ringing up our groceries, mothering our children, and caring for our ailing loved ones, are we ready to stand up for them, knowing there will be a cost? Leng Leng Chancey, the Asian American executive director of 9to5, National Association for Working Women, offered a challenge for this time. She said, "I'm not looking for allies anymore but co-conspirators who take risks."

Epilogue

While finishing the manuscript of this book, Amanda lost her close friend Michele to breast cancer. During two years of intense discussions over tea, Michele had become deeply invested in the contents of this book, talking through chapters and women's stories, partly as distraction from treatment plans and clinical trials. Michele was a pediatric occupational therapist and a lifelong advocate for early childhood and experiential education for all kids, including her two sons. Her husband taught middle school social studies. A middle-class Jewish mother of two, Michele had grown up in Bay Ridge, Brooklyn, and later in life moved to Fairfield County, Connecticut, to raise her family.

Aside from occasional cleaning and babysitting, Michele did not employ much domestic help over the years. As her illness progressed, though, she needed someone to pick up around the house and drive the boys to practice and back. She relied on in-home services—at first housekeepers who would also run errands, and later home health aides—to help her shower, parse medications, and change dressings. Like many people we imagine reading this book, Michele cared deeply about the lives of the women working in her home. She asked about their parents and kids and circumstances. They shared personal information about immigration troubles of family members, a daughter's teenage pregnancy, a car breaking down without up-to-date registration. Michele tried to help, advancing pay or offering vacation time, flexible hours, paid time off, and generous gifts. She passed along contact information of friends and family members with expertise she thought might help.

But in conversations about this book, Michele admitted feeling unsettled by the growing awareness that something deeper was required to change the lives of women like the ones caring intimately for her sons and her body. It is often easier to see the individuals working in our homes and take responsibility for the way that we treat them than to recognize systematic oppression. Though less common, sometimes this feeling of responsibility extends to other low-wage workers we encounter daily, like the affluent mothers refusing to cross the picket line at Stop & Shop stores across New England. These low-wage moms we meet represent so many others we never see, working in the kitchen of fast-food restaurants, delivering groceries to our doorsteps, remembering that extra pump of vanilla syrup in our lattes. Today, low-income and BIPOC women are leading equity movements, but affluent white women who have privilege and resources could be a vital part of those movements.

In the last month of her life, often overwhelmed by pain, Michele expressed a deep desire to be cared for by a particular home health aide, Chevelle. She first met Chevelle, a Black woman in her fifties, through a visiting nurse service. They bonded almost immediately, and Michele's family inquired about scheduling Chevelle on the books through the agency and off the books whenever possible, because they had the resources to do so.

Chevelle would coax Michele to eat another bite of yogurt to keep up her strength for her boys and skillfully maneuver the dressing over a weeping sore so that it wouldn't rub, talking softly the entire time. Chevelle would anticipate her need to shift positions on the couch or later in the hospital bed, lifting and sliding her body with gentle strength. She knew when Michele needed more pain medication or a popsicle to soothe her dry mouth. When Michele stopped being able to get up to go to the bathroom, Chevelle would change soiled bedding before anyone realized, no big deal, transitioning seamlessly between the intimate and the everyday. She whispered to Michele in a way that visibly brought peace and release, singing that everything would be all right, all Michele needed to do was rest. Chevelle demonstrated daily the artistry of skilled personal-care work.

She was a teacher too. Chevelle taught Amanda and the entire family how to be around a loved one who was dying. She was not afraid to press her own forehead up against Michele's feverish skin and to massage her arms and fingers, swollen and stiff. While Michele found comfort in Chevelle's care, Amanda thought a lot about the difference between what we pay homecare workers and what this labor is worth.

During her last weeks, Michele asked constantly when Chevelle could come back. But she also worried that Chevelle was not getting enough sleep and was in danger of losing her health insurance. Because homecare workers seldom have access to benefits, Chevelle also worked nights at a factory job to maintain health insurance for herself and her son. So she would work through the night, stop at home for a few hours, and then drive thirty minutes to Michele's house for a five- or eight-hour shift, then back to the factory and repeat.

Sometimes while working at Michele's house, Chevelle would nod off to sleep, not in a dangerous way while administering medication, but she seemed trained to detect less vital moments of chitchat to drift off, restore, and then return to alertness. Michele constantly encouraged Chevelle to go and take a nap. Get some rest. Eat a sandwich. The kitchen was full, and Michele insisted. Chevelle would watch Michele to make sure she was cared for, and Michele was watching back.

Talking with Amanda, Michele described moving along the pathway from individual compassion to feeling called up to do more. Her illness progressed too quickly for Michele to step into a role of advocacy, but she would have wanted her story to shine a light on the vital issues raised in these pages. To urge readers to stand up in outrage that mothers like Chevelle are routinely paid so little and without benefits to provide the most intimate and important service of our lives.

Chevelle was with Michele when the end came, and in the middle of a night filled with thunder, she held her.

Acknowledgments

We are deeply thankful to the many women who shared their lives with us. Theirs is an essential account of brutal inequity in the United States, of mothers working hard, living poor, and, above all, caring for children. They are the heart of this book. We also want to express deep admiration for the advocates and activists who persist in standing up for working poor women, their families, and their communities. We hope this book will encourage others to join you. Lastly, we would like to express our personal gratitude for our own mothers, sisters, daughters, and granddaughters whose strength, love, and care inspire all that we do.

Notes

Authors' Note

1. Martha Ross and Nicole Bateman, *Meet the Low-Wage Workforce* (Washington, DC: Brookings Institution, 2019), www.brookings.edu /research/meet-the-low-wage-workforce.

2. This book builds on research published in the following co-authored journal article: Amanda Freeman and Lisa Dodson, "Triple Role Overload: Working, Parenting, and Navigating Public Benefits," *Journal of Family Issues* 42, no. 8 (2021): 1737–1761.

1. Girls Step Up

1. Patricia L. East, "Children's Provision of Family Caregiving: Benefit or Burden?" *Child Development Perspectives* 4, no. 1 (April 2010).

2. Abel Valenzuela Jr., "Gender Roles and Settlement Activities Among Children and Their Immigrant Families," *American Behavioral Scientist* 42, no. 4 (January 1999).

3. Amelia Nierenberg, "Meet Genesis, a High School Senior in N.Y.C.," *New York Times*, November 24, 2021.

4. Annette Lareau, *Unequal Childhoods: Class, Race, and Family Life* (Berkeley: University of California Press, 2011).

5. Claire Cain Miller, "The Relentlessness of Modern Parenting," *New York Times*, December 25, 2018.

6. Wendy Luttrell, "Picturing Care: An Introduction," *Gender and Education* 31, no. 5 (2019).

7. Harbour Fraser Hodder, "Girl Power: What Has Changed for Women—and What Hasn't," *Harvard Magazine*, January–February 2008.

8. Heather Koball and Yang Jiang, *Basic Facts About Low-Income Children: Children Under 18 Years, 2016* (New York: National Center for Children in Poverty, 2018), www.nccp.org/publication/basic-facts -about-low-income-children-children-under-18-years-2016.

9. David Cooper, "Workers of Color Are Far More Likely to Be Paid

Poverty-Level Wages Than White Workers," *Economic Policy Institute: Working Economics Blog*, June 21, 2018, www.epi.org/blog/workers -of-color-are-far-more-likely-to-be-paid-poverty-level-wages-than-white -workers.

10. Gretchen Livingston, *The Changing Profile of Unmarried Parents: A Growing Share Are Living Without a Partner*, Pew Research Center, April 25, 2018.

11. Cheridan Christnacht and Briana Sullivan, *About Two-Thirds of the 23.5 Million Working Women with Children Under 18 Worked Full-Time in 2018* (Suitland, MD: U.S. Census Bureau, 2020), www.census .gov/library/stories/2020/05/the-choices-working-mothers-make.html.

12. Angela Hanks, Christian E. Weller, and Danyelle Solomon, *Systematic Inequality: How America's Structural Racism Helped Create the Black-White Wealth Gap* (Washington, DC: Center for American Progress, 2018), www.americanprogress.org/article/systematic-inequality.

13. Emma Ketteringham, "Do Poor Parents Have to Be Perfect?" *New York Times*, August 22, 2017.

2. Shifts to Work Any and All the Time

1. Lawrence Mishel et al., *The State of Working America*, 12th ed. (Ithaca, NY: Cornell University Press, 2012).

2. D. Augustus Anderson and Lynda Laughlin, *Retail Workers 2018: American Community Survey Reports* (Suitland, MD: U.S. Census Bureau, 2020).

3. National Women's Law Center, *When Hard Work Is Not Enough: Women in Low-Paid Jobs* (Washington, DC: National Women's Law Center, 2020).

4. Catherine Ruetschlin and Dedrick Asante-Muhammad, *The Retail Race Divide: How the Retail Industry Is Perpetuating Racial Inequality in the 21st Century* (New York: Demos; and Baltimore: National Association for the Advancement of Colored People, 2015).

5. National Women's Law Center, *When Hard Work Is Not Enough: Women in Low-Paid Jobs*.

6. U.S. Government Accountability Office, *Federal Social Safety Net Programs: Millions of Full-Time Workers Rely on Federal Health Care and Food Assistance Programs* (Washington, DC: U.S. Government Accountability Office, 2020).

7. Nathaniel Meyersohn, "Target Raised Wages. But Some Workers Say Their Hours Were Cut, Leaving Them Struggling," CNN online,

October 14, 2019, www.cnn.com/2019/10/14/business/target-cutting -hours-wage-increase/index.html.

8. Gina Adams, Peter Willenborg, Cary Lou, and Diane Schilder, "To Make the Child Care System More Equitable, Expand Options for Parents Working Nontraditional Hours," *Urban Wire*, January 14, 2021, www .urban.org/urban-wire/make-child-care-system-more-equitable-expand -options-parents-working-nontraditional-hours.

9. Office of Planning, Research and Evaluation, *Fact Sheet: Provision of Early Care and Education During Non-Standard Hours* (Washington, DC.: Office of Planning, Research and Evaluation, 2015), www.acf.hhs .gov/opre/report/fact-sheet-provision-early-care-and-education-during -non-standard-hours.

10. Kim Parker, Juliana Menasce Horowitz, and Rachel Minkin, "How the Coronavirus Outbreak Has—and Hasn't—Changed the Way Americans Work," Pew Research Center, December 9, 2020, www.pewresearch .org/social-trends/2020/12/09/how-the-coronavirus-outbreak-has-and -hasnt-changed-the-way-americans-work.

11. Will Romano, "Amazon's Biggest Exploitation Is Giving Its Workers More Time Off," *Medium* (blog), August 23, 2021, marker.medium .com/amazons-biggest-exploitation-is-giving-its-workers-more-time-off -e0d45dffc39d.

12. One Fair Wage, *Locked Out by Low Wages: Service Workers' Challenges with Accessing Unemployment Insurance During COVID-19* (Berkeley: UC Berkeley Food Labor Research Center, 2020).

13. Denise Mann, "Day Care Babies: More Infections Now, Fewer Later," CNN.com, December 6, 2010, www.cnn.com/2010/HEALTH /12/06/daycare.kids/index.html.

14. Adewale Maye, "Low-Wage Workers Least Likely to Have Paid Sick Days," *Center for Law and Social Policy* (blog), November 21, 2019, www.clasp.org/blog/low-wage-workers-least-likely-have-paid-sick-days.

15. National Partnership for Women & Families, "Most Women in Fast Food Industry Cannot Earn Paid Sick Time, Have Gone to Work with 'Troubling Symptoms,' Survey Finds," press release, November 22, 2016, www.nationalpartnership.org/our-impact/news-room/press-statements /most-women-in-fast-food-industry-cannot-earn-paid-sick-time-have -gone-to-work-with-troubling-symptoms-survey-finds.html.

16. Bridget Ansel and Matt Markezich, *Falling Behind the Rest of the World: Childcare in the United States* (Washington, DC: Washington Center for Equitable Growth, 2017), equitablegrowth.org/falling-behind -the-rest-of-the-world-childcare-in-the-united-states.

17. Claire Cain Miller, "Walmart and Now Starbucks: Why More Big

Companies Are Offering Paid Family Leave," *New York Times*, January 24, 2018.

18. U.S. Bureau of Labor Statistics, *Employee Benefits Survey* (Washington, DC: U.S. Bureau of Labor Statistics, 2018), www.bls.gov /ncs/ebs/benefits/2018/home.htm.

19. Alana Semuels, "Poor at 20, Poor for Life," *Atlantic*, July 14, 2016.

20. Todd Gabe, Jaison R. Abel, and Richard Florida, *Can Low-Wage Workers Find Better Jobs?* (New York City: Federal Reserve Bank of New York, 2018), www.newyorkfed.org/research/staff_reports/sr846.

3. Care Work for Cheap

1. Stephen Campbell et al., *Caring for the Future: The Power and Potential of America's Direct Care Workforce* (New York City: PHI, 2021), phinational.org/resource/caring-for-the-future-the-power-and -potential-of-americas-direct-care-workforce.

2. Julia Wolfe et al., *Domestic Workers Chartbook* (Washington, DC: Economic Policy Institute, 2020), www.epi.org/publication/domestic -workers-chartbook-a-comprehensive-look-at-the-demographics-wages -benefits-and-poverty-rates-of-the-professionals-who-care-for-our-family -members-and-clean-our-homes.

3. Lauren Hilgers, "Out of the Shadows," *New York Times Magazine*, February 24, 2019.

4. Mikki Kendall, *Hood Feminism: Notes from the Women That a Movement Forgot* (New York: Penguin, 2021).

5. Domestic Workers Bill of Rights Act, H.R. 4826, 117th Cong., 2021–2022.

6. Diana Boesch and Shilpa Phadke, *When Women Lose All the Jobs: Essential Actions for Gender-Equitable Recovery* (Washington, DC: Center for American Progress, 2021), www.americanprogress.org/article /women-lose-jobs-essential-actions-gender-equitable-recovery.

4. The Centrality of Motherhood

1. Kathryn Edin and Maria J. Kefalas, *Promises I Can Keep: Why Poor Women Put Motherhood Before Marriage* (Berkeley: University of California Press, 2005).

2. Rosanna Hertz, Jane Mattes, and Alexandria Shook, "When Paid Work Invades the Family: Single Mothers in the COVID-19 Pandemic," *Journal of Family Issues* 42, no. 9 (2021): 2019–45.

3. U.S. Census Bureau, *44 Percent of Custodial Parents Receive the*

Full Amount of Child Support (Washington, DC: U.S. Census Bureau, 2018), www.census.gov/newsroom/press-releases/2018/cb18-tps03.html.

4. U.S. Chamber of Commerce Foundation, *Childcare: An Essential Industry for Economic Recovery* (Washington, DC: U.S. Chamber of Commerce Foundation, 2020).

5. Lillian Mongeau, "After Mass Closures, Too Little Support, Post-Pandemic Child Care Options Will Be Scarce," *Hechinger Report* online, February 16, 2021, hechingerreport.org/after-mass-closures-too-little -support-post-pandemic-child-care-options-will-be-scarce.

6. Steven Jessen-Howard and Simon Workman, "Coronavirus Pandemic Could Lead to Permanent Loss of Nearly 4.5 Million Child Care Slots," *Center for American Progress* online, April 24, 2020, www .americanprogress.org/article/coronavirus-pandemic-lead-permanent-loss -nearly-4-5-million-child-care-slots.

7. Gretchen Livingston, "Stay-at-Home Moms and Dads Account for About One-in-Five U.S. Parents," *Pew Research Center* online, September 24, 2018, www.pewresearch.org/fact-tank/2018/09/24/stay-at-home -moms-and-dads-account-for-about-one-in-five-u-s-parents.

8. U.S. Census Bureau, *Quick Facts: Westchester County, New York* (Washington, DC: U.S. Census Bureau, 2020), www.census.gov /quickfacts/fact/table/westchestercountynewyork/LFE046219.

9. Julia Wolfe, "Domestic Workers Are at Risk During the Coronavirus Crisis," *Economic Policy Institute: Working Economics Blog*, April 8, 2020, www.epi.org/blog/domestic-workers-are-at-risk-during -the-coronavirus-crisis-data-show-most-domestic-workers-are-black -hispanic-or-asian-women.

10. Lila MacLellan, "70% of Top Male Earners in the US Have a Spouse Who Stays Home," *Quartz at Work* online, April 30, 2019, qz.com/work /1607995/most-men-in-the-top-1-of-us-earners-have-a-spouse-who-stays -home.

11. Laura A. Schifter et al., *Students from Low-Income Families and Special Education* (New York: The Century Foundation, 2019), tcf .org/content/report/students-low-income-families-special-education/? session=1.

12. Mikki Kendall, *Hood Feminism: Notes from the Women That a Movement Forgot* (New York: Penguin, 2021).

5. The Broken Promise of Childcare

1. Peter T. Kilborn and Sam Howe Verhovek, "Welfare Shift Reflects New Democrats," *New York Times*, August 2, 1996.

2. Julie Blair, "Only 42 Percent of Eligible Children Participate in Head Start," *Education Week* online, November 25, 2013, www.edweek.org /policy-politics/only-42-percent-of-eligible-children-participate-in-head -start/2013/11.

3. Bridget Ansel and Matt Markezich, *Falling Behind the Rest of the World: Childcare in the United States.*

4. Pia Rebello Britto, Hirokazu Yoshikawa, and Kimberly Boller, "Quality of Early Childhood Development Programs in Global Contexts: Rationale for Investment, Conceptual Framework and Implications for Equity," *Society for Research in Child Development* 25, no. 2 (2011).

5. Mary King, "A New National Model for Preschool and Child Care in the U.S.," *Inequality.org* online, March 3, 2021, inequality.org/research /universal-childcare-portland.

6. Elise Gould, *Child Care Workers Aren't Paid Enough to Make Ends Meet* (Washington, DC: Economic Policy Institute, 2015), www.epi.org /publication/child-care-workers-arent-paid-enough-to-make-ends-meet.

7. Douglas Rice, Stephanie Schmit, and Hannah Matthews, *Child Care and Housing: Big Expenses with Too Little Help Available* (Washington, DC: Center on Budget and Policy Priorities, 2019), www.cbpp.org /research/housing/child-care-and-housing-big-expenses-with-too-little -help-available.

8. María E. Enchautegui, *Nonstandard Work Schedules and the Well-Being of Low-Income Families* (Washington, DC: Urban Institute, 2013).

9. Yasmina Vinci and David Medina, "Opinion: America's Early Education System Is Struggling. Head Start Can Help Chart a Path Forward," *The Hechinger Report* online, May 24, 2021, hechingerreport .org/opinion-americas-early-education-system-is-struggling-head-start -can-help-chart-a-path-forward.

10. Julie Kashen, Sarah Jane Glynn, and Amanda Novello, *How COVID-19 Sent Women's Workforce Progress Backward* (Washington, DC: Center for American Progress, 2020), www.americanprogress.org /article/covid-19-sent-womens-workforce-progress-backward.

11. Michael Karpman et al., *The COVID-19 Pandemic Is Straining Families' Abilities to Afford Basic Needs* (Washington, DC: Urban Institute, 2020).

12. Jen Christensen, "The Pandemic Has Pushed Children's Mental Health and Access to Care to a 'Crisis Point,'" *CNN* online, July 22, 2021, cnn.com/2021/07/22/health/covid-19-pandemic-mental-health -children/index.html.

6. Moms and Kids on a Cliff

1. Ife Floyd et al., *TANF Policies Reflect Racist Legacy of Cash Assistance* (Washington, DC: Center on Budget and Policy Priorities, 2021), www.cbpp.org/research/family-income-support/tanf-policies-reflect-racist-legacy-of-cash-assistance.

2. Kalena Thomhave, "Battle Over TANF Family Cap Intensifies," *Spotlight on Poverty and Opportunity* online, October 3, 2018, spotlightonpoverty.org/spotlight-exclusives/battle-over-tanf-family-cap-intensifies.

3. Vishakha Agarwal, Brandynn Holgate, Randy Albelda, Caitlin Carey, and Susan R. Crandall, "Cliff Effect Simulations for Families in Suffolk County, Massachusetts: Exploring the Impact of Universal Childcare and Housing Assistance," policy brief, Center for Social Policy McCormack Graduate School for Policy and Global Studies, October 30, 2018.

4. Dhaval M. Dave, Hope Corman, and Nancy E. Reichman, "Effects of Welfare Reform on Education Acquisition of Adult Women," *Journal of Labor Research* 33, no. 2 (2012).

5. Pamela J. Loprest, *How Has the TANF Caseload Changed over Time?* (Washington, DC: Urban Institute, 2012).

6. Kathryn J. Edin and H. Luke Shaefer, "20 Years Since Welfare 'Reform,'" *Atlantic*, August 22, 2016.

7. Robert A. Moffitt, *From Welfare to Work: What the Evidence Shows* (Washington, DC: Brookings Institution, 2002).

8. "2020 Estimated Improper Payment Rates for Centers for Medicare & Medicaid Services (CMS) Programs," *Centers for Medicare and Medicaid Services* online, November 16, 2020, www.cms.gov/newsroom/fact-sheets/2020-estimated-improper-payment-rates-centers-medicare-medicaid-services-cms-programs.

9. Linda Carroll, "Even in the U.S., Poor Women Often Can't Afford Tampons, Pads," *Reuters* online, January 10, 2019, www.reuters.com/article/us-health-menstruation-usa/even-in-the-u-s-poor-women-often-cant-afford-tampons-pads-idUSKCN1P42TX.

7. Keeping Us in Our Place

1. Barbara Gault, Tessa Holtzman, and Lindsey Reichlin Cruse, *Understanding the Student Parent Experience: The Need for Improved Data Collection on Parent Status in Higher Education* (Washington, DC: Institute for Women's Policy Research, 2020).

2. David Radwin et al., *2022–12 National Postsecondary Student Aid Study* (Washington, DC: National Center for Education Statistics, 2013).

3. Amanda L. Freeman, "Moving 'Up and Out' Together: Exploring the Mother-Child Bond in Low-Income, Single-Mother-Headed Families," *Journal of Marriage and Family* 79, no. 3 (2016).

4. Eleanor Eckerson et al., *Child Care for Parents in College: A State-by-State Assessment* (Washington, DC: Institute for Women's Policy Research, 2016).

5. Emma Whitford, "'Time Poverty' of Students Who Are Parents," *Inside Higher Ed* online, October 2, 2018, www.insidehighered.com /news/2018/10/02/student-parents-complete-degrees-more-slowly-drop -out-due-time-poverty.

6. Amanda Freeman, "The Winding Path to Degree: Obstacles to Higher Education for Low-Income Single Mothers," *Journal of Women and Gender in High Education* 13, no. 3 (2020); Rachel Karp, *Why We Should Invest in Single Mothers' Higher Education* (Washington, DC: Institute for Women's Policy Research, 2018).

7. Amanda Freeman, "Colleges Aren't Very Kid-Friendly," *Atlantic*, October 13, 2016.

8. Institute for Women's Policy Research, *Women Gain Jobs in Construction Trades but Remain Underrepresented in the Field* (Washington DC: Institute for Women's Policy Research, 2019).

9. "Single Parenting and Today's Family," *American Psychological Association* online, October 31, 2019, www.apa.org/topics/parenting /single-parent.

8. Calling Us Up

1. Alyssa Fowers and Shelly Tan, "The New Sick Leave Law Doesn't Help the Workers That Need It Most," *Washington Post*, March 19, 2020.

2. Molly Kinder and Laura Stateler, *Amazon and Walmart Have Raked in Billions in Additional Profits During the Pandemic, and Shared Almost None of It with Their Workers* (Washington, DC: Brookings Institution, 2020), www.brookings.edu/blog/the-avenue/2020/12/22/amazon -and-walmart-have-raked-in-billions-in-additional-profits-during-the -pandemic-and-shared-almost-none-of-it-with-their-workers.

3. Adie Tomer and Joseph W. Kane, *To Protect Frontline Workers During and After COVID-19, We Must Define Who They Are* (Washington, DC: Brookings Institution, 2020), www.brookings.edu/research/to -protect-frontline-workers-during-and-after-covid-19-we-must-define -who-they-are.

4. Daniel Flaming, Peter Dreier, Patrick Burns, and Aaron Danielson, *Hungry at the Table: White Paper on Grocery Workers at the Kroger Company* (Los Angeles, CA: Economic Roundtable, 2022).

5. Guy Maddalone, "Advising Clients Hiring Household Help During the Coronavirus Pandemic," *Accounting Today* online, July 14, 2020, www.accountingtoday.com/opinion/advising-clients-hiring-household -help-during-the-coronavirus-pandemic.

6. Alana Samuels, "The Epicenter of American Inequality," *Atlantic*, September 23, 2016.

Index

About the Authors

Lisa Dodson is Research Professor Emerita at Boston College. She is the author of *The Moral Underground: How Ordinary Americans Subvert an Unfair Economy* and *Don't Call Us Out of Name: The Untold Lives of Women and Girls in Poor America*. She lives in Portland, Oregon.

Amanda Freeman is an assistant professor of sociology at the University of Hartford and a writer and researcher of motherhood and work. She lives in Westport, Connecticut. This is her first book.

Other Titles of Interest from The New Press

*The Age of Dignity: Preparing for the Elder Boom
in a Changing America*
Ai-Jen Poo

*The Fight for Fifteen: The Right Wage
for a Working America*
David Rolf

*From the Folks Who Brought You the Weekend:
An Illustrated History of Labor in the United States*
Priscilla Murolo and A.B. Chitty
with illustrations by Joe Sacco

A History of America in Ten Strikes
Eric Loomis

*In a Day's Work: The Fight to End Sexual Violence Against
America's Most Vulnerable Workers*
Bernice Yeung

*Labor Rising: The Past and Future
of Working People in America*
Daniel Katz and Richard A. Greenwald

One Fair Wage: Ending Subminimum Pay in America
Saru Jayaraman

Thick: And Other Essays
Tressie McMillan Cottom

Under the Bus: How Working Women Are Being Run Over
Caroline Fredrickson

We Own the Future: Democratic Socialism—American Style
edited by Michael Kazin, Kate Aronoff, and Peter Dreier

*Working: People Talk About What They Do All Day
and How They Feel About What They Do*
Studs Terkel

*Working-Class New York:
Life and Labor Since World War II*
Joshua B. Freeman

Publishing in the Public Interest

Thank you for reading this book published by The New Press. The New Press is a nonprofit, public interest publisher. New Press books and authors play a crucial role in sparking conversations about the key political and social issues of our day.

We hope you enjoyed this book and that you will stay in touch with The New Press. Here are a few ways to stay up to date with our books, events, and the issues we cover:

- Sign up at www.thenewpress.com/subscribe to receive updates on New Press authors and issues and to be notified about local events
- Facebook: www.facebook.com/newpressbooks
- Twitter: www.twitter.com/thenewpress
- Instagram: www.instagram.com/thenewpress

Please consider buying New Press books for yourself; for friends and family; or to donate to schools, libraries, community centers, prison libraries, and other organizations involved with the issues our authors write about.

The New Press is a 501(c)(3) nonprofit organization. You can also support our work with a tax-deductible gift by visiting www.thenewpress.com/donate.